Editorial

On 14 June 1986 – just over a quarter of a century ago – the Argentinian writer Jorge Luis Borges died in Geneva. He is a figure who has haunted *PN Review* since it took its first steps as *Poetry Nation I*. He remains with us, his poems and fictions reviving their more than enigmatic ironies.

A sonnet from 1964 entitled 'Un Poeta del Siglo XIII' ('A Poet of the Thirteenth Century') sees the poet looking through the crumpled drafts of his poem. It is about to become the very first, as yet unrecognised, sonnet. In his drafts Borges' poet has mixed quatrains and tercets, not yet quite regular. He labours on a further draft, then hesitates:

> 'Acaso le ha llegado
> del porvenir y de su horror sagrado
> un rumor de remotos ruiseñores.'

Perhaps he has sensed, says the poem, radiating *from the future*, 'a rumour of far-off nightingales'. Of things to come, a suggestion of a new form and maybe (a step beyond it) of impending clichés. The modern poet asks, in the sonnet's sestet:

> ¿Habrá sentido que no estaba solo
> y que el arcáno, el increible Apolo
> le habia revelado un arquetipo,
>
> un ávido cristal que apresaría
> cuanto la noche cierra y abre el dia:
> dédalo, laberinto, enigma, Edipo?

('Had he detected he was not alone, / that the cryptic, the unimaginable Apollo / had disclosed to him an archetypal pattern, // a greedy crystal that would capture, / the way night closes day opens it: / Dedalus, labyrinth, the riddle, Laius son.')

In Borges's poem the future weighs on the present, just as the past can do: in looking back, we see a past aware of our gaze, returning it. Inherencies, less a promise than an earnest. Once that first sonnet is recognised by its poet, not as a discovery but as a thing given by 'the unimaginable Apollo', once it is in language and the form defined, a course is set. This sonnet, we understand from Apollo and from the last line, works with anciencies. Classical myth, legend, literature – common memories – provide the content. The thirteenth-century poet, suspended between a pre-classical *then* and a post-modern *now*, mediates. Each later sonnet in whatever language participates in his work, and he in its.

A poet who develops received forms is always in collaboration with the poems that came before and those that will come after. A sonnet never belongs exclusively to its author. Or even to its language.

In the 1960s Borges started collecting the 'milongas' he had been composing, including several in 1965 in *Para las Seis Cuerdas* (*For the Six Strings*) – a reference to the six strings of the *guitarrón argentino*. In his preface he asks the reader to imagine, in the absence of music, a strumming singer in a shadowy passage or a shop. His hand lingers on the strings, words count for less than imagined harmonies. This is a new kind of poem, though familiar as song; it really ought to date from the 1890s, when the form was popular, ingenious and spirited. Borges's modern versions are, he says, elegies, aftermaths of a form and a once vital popular culture. Though the poems are formally original, they are not *his*. In a recorded comment he declares, 'The milongas I shall recite wrote themselves, almost against my will. Better said, they were composed by the dead creoles who wander through my blood. The names, the stories that these milongas tell are true.'

What is true is that the milonga never belongs definitively to its author, even if he was the first to make of it a literary form. In composing his milongas, Borges collaborates with a musical form and a narrative, ballad-like tradition, although more urban in cast. This erudite poet-librarian, who was put in charge of Argentina's national library in the year in which he went blind, steps away from his usual concerns into the streets of his city, the musically tuned heart of a tradition. A self-effacing, enchanting collaboration ensues.

At the birth of the sonnet, *a net is woven*. It is a net that can be used to snare all sorts of quarries. In the thirteenth and the twenty-first century the sonnet remains serviceable. And the milonga remains serviceable too, though it belongs specifically to Spanish, and to Argentinean Spanish.

When David Jones, quoting Nennius, makes a heap of all he can find in the *Anathemata*; or Eliot makes a heap of broken images, quoting *Ecclesiastes*, in 'The Waste Land', with material drawn from many sources, both enter into complex collaborations. For Eliot these collaborations intersect with his real-time collaboration with Pound and Vivienne. The original works, fragments of which are given new context in Eliot's poem, have as much a claim on his poem as his does on theirs. It is a matter of participation rather than appropriation. It would take a reader with a most fastidious sense of copyright to resist the incorporation of earlier material in a poem. Does anyone object to George Herbert using a line of Sir Philip Sidney's: 'Let me not love thee if I love thee not'? Or the collaboration of Doctor Johnson in Goldsmith's 'The Deserted Village', namely the closing lines?

Gertrude Stein was a new kind of collaborator. Her forty-page meditation on Henry James, for example, entitled 'Henry James' and composed towards the start of the 1930s, is first about Shakespeare, then about her own practice in the poem 'Before the Flowers of Friendship Faded Friendship Faded', and only then, and obliquely, about Henry James at all. She begins with a question: 'What is the difference between Shakespeare's plays and Shakespeare's sonnets.' (This keeps us conveniently in the zone of the sonnet.) Immediately she moves on to distinguish between accident, which her discovery was, and coincidence, which it also was. 'An accident is when a thing happens. A coincidence is when a thing is going to happen and it does.' Having set these contrasts in motion, she composes what she subtitles a 'Duet'. This is how 'Duet' begins:

> And so it is not an accident but a coincidence that there is a difference between Shakespeare's sonnets and Shakespeare's plays. The coincidence is with Before the Flowers of Friendship Faded Friendship Faded.
> Who knew that the answer was going to be like that. Had I told that the answer was going to be like that?
> The answer is not like that. The answer is that.
> I am I not any longer when I see.
> This sentence is at the bottom of all creative activity. It is just the opposite of I am I because my little dog knows me.

She has *seen* something about her poem 'Before the Flowers of Friendship Faded Friendship Faded' that takes it away from her composing 'I' and puts it in the company of other work that has shed the composing 'I'. What strikes her about her poem and Shakespeare's Sonnets is this: 'Shakespeare's plays were written as they were written. Shakespeare's sonnets were written as they were going to be written.' The earnest that was there in Borges's first sonneteer's first sonnet is fulfilled, for the n-th time, in Shakespeare's sonnets.

It is like chasing a butterfly with a net – not a sonnet – to read Stein's seeming-babble for sense. The key distinction she makes between writers is this: 'They either write as they write or they write as they are going to write and they may not choose to do what they are going to do.' And what does Stein understand when she says 'see' – *I am I not any longer when I see*? She is not talking about a thing seen, the image as writers construe it nowadays, reportage, out there in the world, which must be got precise and right in words. Her *see* sees not a thing but, when there has been a specific occasion – a tree, say, or a beautiful face, or a lovers' argument, or a painting – sees *it* and not its occasion. Her *see* sees, despite external point of view and occasion. The seen is no longer 'hers', it is itself, made, and in its own time, the time Borges imagines with such plasticity... I am put in mind of a familiar formulation, 'it takes its origin from emotion recollected in tranquility: the emotion is contemplated till, by a species of reaction, the tranquility gradually disappears, and an emotion, kindred to that which was before the subject of contemplation, is gradually produced, and does itself actually exist in the mind.' The activity is not secondary, memory; it is primary. The reader's activity, too, is primary: 'if his Reader's mind be sound and vigorous'. The poem's action is not just historical, a moment, the record of something: it adds to available reality.

News and Notes

Friederike Mayröcker

Jena Schmitt writes: The Austrian writer Friederike Mayröcker died on June 4, 2021, at the age of 96. Since her first poems appeared in the journal *Plan* in 1946, she published over one hundred books of poetry, prose, librettos, plays, radio plays, children's books and hybrid in-between formats, collaborating with writers and artists including her partner, the poet Ernst Jandl (1925–2000), and winning such prestigious awards as the Austrian Prize for Literature and the Georg Büchner Prize. 'I went from a purely experimental writing to a kind of narrational writing, though in interviews I have always declined to label my writing as storytelling,' she said in a 1983 interview with Siegfried J. Schmidt. 'I don't want to write stories in any usual sense, but I want to approach a totally unconventional, unorthodox narrational writing, if one can call it that.' Her experiments with form, genre, syntax, semantics, punctuation, grammar and quotation have led to a dazzlingly evocative and innovative array of texts, ravelments filled with memories, feelings, artistic influences, reminiscences both real and imagined, an accordion-like overlapping of time and place, of the *Umwelt* or "world around" her and a rich inner landscape. Mayröcker's most recent collections include *Pathos und Schwalbe* (2018) and *da ich morgens und moosgrün. Ans Fenster trete* (2020), and the English translations *Requiem for Ernst Jandl* (2018), *Scardanelli* (2018), études (2020), *just sitting around here GRUESOMELY now* (2021) and *The Communicating Vessels* (2021), in which she wrote (in Alexander Booth's translation): '...and I sink down and my throat is tied and I wiped the blood out of my hair, and now the end has come, but I have not found an end I never find an end...'

(An extended essay on Mayröcker's work, by Jena Schmitt, is scheduled for publication in *PN Review*.)

Francisco Brines

Michael Schmidt writes: At a literary conference in Valencia in the 1980s I bought a book of poems by Francisco Brines, a writer I had not heard of before. I loved the poems and in my enthusiasm shared it with my neighbour. He blushed and turned aside. Later in the proceeding someone told me, 'That's Francisco Brines.'

He is the most recent recipient of the Cervantes Prize (the most important of the Spanish literary awards), celebrated and not yet sufficiently translated across the world. He was born in Valencia in 1932 and died in Oliva, not far from the landscape of his childhood, *El Mundo* reminded its readers. His life was devoted, the obituarist declared, 'to writing, hedonism and friendship'.

Though Valencia was his home, he spent part of the Spanish Civil War in Marseilles. Still a boy, he came home to a happy youth, and his life was inflected by those years and the loss that their passing represented. In 2020 he said in an interview that most of his writing proceeded from that sense of loss, his poetry evoking at one and the same time the joy and happiness of that earlier time and the loss. They are part and parcel of one another, the positive and the negative held in tension. His early writings date from his student years in the Law departments of Deusto, Valencia and finally Salamanca, and then Madrid where he studied Philosophy and Literature. His first book – published when he was twenty-eight – was awarded the Adonais Prize. Clearly he was not in a great hurry. He had taken his bearings from some of the great poets of the generations before his, Cernuda in particular, and made his way not by contrariety but by continuation and extension. He spent much of his time in Madrid, living among poets but also making his writing way independently of the movements and fashions of the time. His sensuality and subtle eroticism develop, darken and deepen in an *oeuvre* that is coherent and abundant. His prosody is beautiful to follow, full of unexpected but always effective turns, surprises and climaxes. His first collected poems appeared in 1974: *An Attempt at Farewell*. He was a great reader of poems and a brilliant critic. He looked always for pleasure, and when he found it he spoke if its various qualities. His enthusiasms were broad, he was a tolerant man and a tolerant critic, keen to be surprised out of himself.

Seamus Deane

John McAuliffe writes: The Irish critic, novelist and poet Seamus Deane has died at the age of eighty-one. He was the most formidable Irish critic of his generation, a scholar of Edmund Burke and the author of acute, elegant studies such as *Celtic Revivals* and *A Short History of Modern Irish Literature*. He was also a talker and lecturer of prodigious ability, memorious and articulate not just on Burke and Joyce, Derek Mahon and T.S. Eliot but also on Durkheim and Daniel O'Connell and, the obituaries published by friends, former colleagues and students in the *Irish Times* attest, a wide range of non-academic subjects too.

Deane grew up in the Bogside in Derry, which is the subject of his Booker-shortlisted novel *Reading in* the Dark, a book which began as a memoir until he found, as he told one interviewer, that he could no longer tell his own stories apart from those he had heard from others. He studied at St Columb's College in Derry, a 'scholarship boy' from a brilliant generation that included Seamus Heaney, Brian Friel and John Hume. After taking a BA at Queens he completed his PhD at Cambridge and initially taught at Berkeley before taking up a post at UCD.

There, he directed the theatrical and publishing activities of Field Day, which would include the Derry premiere of Friel's *Translations*, a series of pamphlets which brought Irish Studies firmly into the ambit of international post-colonial theory, and the massive editorial project *The Field Day Anthology*, whose initial three volumes established a new way of considering Irish literary history and culture, while also creating a controversy about gender which has, perhaps, been as influential as that work's monumental scholarship. In the wake of the anthology's publication, Deane was challenged to explain its omissions by interviewers such as Nuala O'Faolain and by Eavan Boland's comment that she was 'sorry to be included'. He acknowledged immediately the need for 'a correction of the error against feminism that percolates through the anthology' and his colleague Geraldine Meaney has recognised 'the intellectual integrity [in how] he worked to redress this in commissioning two further volumes on women's writings and traditions'.

Deane's other work included a *Selected Poems* (Gallery, 1988), essays most recently collected in *Small World: Ireland, 1798–2018* and the editorship of the beautifully produced journal, *Field Day Review,* published from his last academic post at the University of Notre Dame.

Chris 'Zithulele' Mann

Chris Miller writes: The South African poet, singer, and song-writer Chris 'Zithulele' Mann died in Makhanda/Grahamstown on 10 March 2021. I have met few men I admired more. Born in 1948, he took a BA at Wits University, followed by an Oxford MA

in English Language and Literature and one from SOAS in African Oral Literature. Returning to SA, he worked for twelve years in rural development. In 1999, he founded Wordfest, a festival celebrating the many South African languages of poetry. As a singer, he performed illegally in multiracial groups under Apartheid, and at Mandela's first post-release rally, before an audience of a quarter of a million. He was constantly inventing new ways of making poetry accessible. His poems are one long description of South Africa, but his most personal volume is *Rudiments of Grace* (2014), dedicated to his wife, the artist Julia Skeen, and movingly retracing the course of their shared lives and love. His was a life dedicated to South Africa, to patient work, often against the odds, to improve the lives of his fellow citizens. To help him do this, he built a body of thought and poetry (see *PNR* 209 for an essay on him). In this thought, the notion of the 'shade' carried a singular importance, the Nguni notion of ancestor shades expanded to include all the dead who continue to influence us, from parents to Virgil. In person, he was short, stocky, thoughtful and modest, his love of life an aspect of the askesis by which he lived in the service of others, constantly grateful for what he had been given and humbly anxious to give back. Poetry and an inclusive Christianity were his two faiths wrought into one. He was deeply saddened by what post-Mandela SA had become but committed to the work of reconciliation. He died peacefully, surrounded by his loved ones. When last I spoke to him, he showed me with delight the flowers growing behind his house. I knew he had had cancer but had no idea he was dying. His courage seemed, as always, undimmed, and he was writing almost to the last.

Brian Johnstone of StAnza

In May we learned with much sadness of the death of Brian Johnstone. He was a founder of StAnza Poetry Festival in 1998 and Festival Director from 2000 to 2010 – a key figure in its evolution. He was also a poet in his own right, a well-known reader of his

work at home and abroad and widely translated into other languages. 'In 2015, in recognition of his contribution to the organisation, he was appointed Honorary President. StAnza owes Brian a huge debt and he is remembered with fondness and gratitude by those at StAnza who worked with him from 1997 until 2020.'

Eleanor Livingstone worked with Brian as Artistic Director and from 2010 as his successor as Festival Director. She found in him an excellent mentor. 'I was fortunate in inheriting the relationships he had established – with funders and partners, with venues and the many businesses whose cooperation underpinned the festival's success – and the procedures and processes he had designed and initiated.' Robyn Marsack spoke of his later years: 'Free of his director's responsibilities, he was glad to focus on his own work – in prose, poetry and musical collaborations – and indeed launched a new collection in April, *The Marks on the Map*, when dozens of friends were gathered online to celebrate the occasion.'

Premio Reina Sofía de Poesía Iberoamericana

The thirtieth Queen Sofia award for Iberoamerican Poetry – the highest award for Spanish and Portuguese-language poetry, went to the Portuguese-language poet and feminist critic Ana Luisa Amaral, born in Lisbon in 1956. The Patrimonio Nacional de España and Salamanca University jointly fund the prize which is valued at 42,100 euros. The poet spoke of her tremendous joy and pride at the receipt of the prize which entails writers from all the countries of the Iberian peninsula and the colonies of Spain and Portugal. In Amaral's poetry, above all, the award presentation noted, 'the voice of woman can be clearly heard', a 'quite extraordinary woman'.

Amaral is a professor at the University of Oporto, where she took her doctorate in the poetry of Emily Dickinson. She has published widely on British and American poetry and in comparative literature and feminist theory.

Pigott Prize

Eiléan Ní Chuilleanáin was awarded the €10,000 Pigott Poetry Prize (the largest poetry money-prize in Ireland) for *Collected Poems*. The selectors, Maura Dooley and Mark Waldron, said that the book, published by Gallery, was 'of singular beauty and uncommon cohesion. It contains work from more than fifty years – nine collections and new previously unpublished poems. For all the serenity of their surfaces a core of historical concern permeates her lines. Often she attends to marginalised or solitary figures, and embraces multiple journeys which transport her readers to the dramas of hinted narratives.' Mark Pigott, who sponsors the prize, is executive chairman of Paccar, who also recently donated £200,000, which Queen's University Belfast matched, to endow a £400,000 Michael Longley Scholarship Fund for postgraduate students and to create a classroom known as the Longley Room, recognising two lifetimes of poetry excellence: Michael Longley's, and his wife, Professor Edna Longley's.

Forward Prize

The Forward Prizes announced their shortlist as representing a 'perfect slice of the now'. It honours the work of the independent presses. The three shortlists are:

Best Collection (£10,000)
A Blood Condition, Kayo Chingonyi (Chatto). *A God at the Door*, Tishani Doshi (Bloodaxe). *Men Who Feed Pigeons*, Selima Hill (Bloodaxe). *Notes on the Sonnets*, Luke Kennard (Penned in the Margins). *Cheryl's Destinies*, Stephen Sexton (Penguin).

Felix Dennis Prize for Best First Collection (£5,000)
Poor, Caleb Femi (Penguin). *bird of winter*, Alice Hiller (Pavillion Poetry). *Honorifics*, Cynthia Miller (Nine Arches). *Comic Timing*, Holly Pester (Granta). *Rotten Days in Late Summer*, Ralf Webb (Penguin).

Best Single Poem (£1,000)
'Androgeus', Fiona Benson (*Times Literary Supplement*). 'Middle Name with Diacritics', Natalie Linh Bolderstone (National Poetry Competition). 'Flower of Sulphur', John McCullough (*Poetry London*). '1948', Denise Riley (*Poetry Ireland Review*). 'Pages 22–29, an excerpt from the Ferguson Report: An Erasure', Nicole Sealey (*Poetry London*)

Stuff and Nonsense
J. Kates

To Mr. Kates:

I am drawing your attention to the misogynistic nature of the subject line of your email of April 18, 2021, and to its threatening overtones. Both the New Hampshire Attorney General's Office and the NH State Troopers have been alerted of [sic] *your email. I do not welcome any future communication from you; if you fail to observe this request, I will consider contacting art and writing agencies in the state and in reference to your behavior.*

The e-mail arrived on my desk on May 21. It was signed, but I am not identifying the sender here. At first, I had no idea what it referred to. Then I remembered that I had queried the writer, a local poet whom I have never met or communicated with before, about a typographical error in one of her poems. My note to her did not originate from my own mail account, but from her web-site "contact" link, and therefore left no record in my own files. Still, I couldn't imagine anything heinous enough to generate such a response after a month of silence.

An old friend I knew was acquainted with the sender. I forwarded the e-mail to her, and asked her to ask N for an explanation. But my friend's immediate response (by telephone) was, 'Oh, that was you! N had been in touch with me a month ago to complain about a stalker who threatened to behead her! But she didn't mention any name.' N had apparently then been so traumatised by my threat that she quivered silently for a month.

Our mutual friend offered to go between.

At the mention of beheading, though, a penny dropped. The ambiguity of the possible typo I had questioned at the beginning was between the words *axe* and *axle* – certainly evoking different images in N's poem. That led me to remember that I might have used in the subject line the words (marked as quotation with appropriate punctuation) from *Alice in Wonderland*: "Talking of axes, off with her head."

I needn't wait for a SWAT team to come busting through my door, though, ready to confiscate all sharp objects. According to my intermediary friend, N had not named anyone in her report to the constabulary. She just told the State Police that she was in imminent danger of being decapitated, presumably – if her note to me is to be taken at face value – because she is a woman.

Conscientiously, I ran the record of this incident by several women, including college students who have and have not read Lewis Carroll carefully, my wife (an immigrant who has read *Alice* only in Nabokov's translation, which botches the line) and others who can glibly quote whole stretches of the book. The unanimous reaction has been unqualified laughter.

Nevertheless, according to our mutual friend, N continues to see no ambiguity in this, feels no need to backtrack, and wants no communication with me.

Three things have come out of this. First, an anecdote I can dine out on for months.

Second, the unsolicited testimonials to my good character by two people (one of whom I hardly know at all) who have sent their own notes to N.

Third, an as yet undefined uneasiness that some seriousness must underlie all this, if only I could tease out what it is.

In the meanwhile, what does disturb me most about the whole affair is that N teaches at a reputable university.

What I enjoy most is N's threat to take her case to a far Higher Authority than the legal and police apparatus of the state: *arts organisations*.

Reports

Report from Edinburgh
Connexion and Shredding
VAHNI CAPILDEO

Edinburgh is a city of many levels. If you dip down to the level of disused rail tracks, you access a network of paths and junctions with names that seem ancient (Fiveways, Goldenacre) but may date back only a couple of hundred years, or as recently as the 1980s, when the local trains went out of use. Bluebells (pinkbells, whitebells) linger on the cool and shady slopes weeks after their kindred have gone to earth in the south. Under one of the dripping bridges, graffiti, and installations memorialised Sarah Everard's tragic death. There is no mention of the neighbourhood murder, fourteen years ago, which saw another woman dismembered, left in bags (not all of which have been recovered) along these stretches that invite us to walk their invention of pastoral. I wonder if one name – a new name every few years – can stand in for all of them; all of us. High up between the young mixed trees, a string sculpture stretches airily across the pathway, creating a sense of a threshold. Bat enthusiasts have signposted a bat trail. Good dogs bound and abound. Some walkers litter-pick as they go along, proud to maintain their environment. Viewing the green ways from above, would you see connexion or shredding?

Litter picking, like foraging, is a mild form of the greater housework that we undertake as inhabitants of (or passengers through) a place. Gathering is something else again. Edinburgh writer Alice Tarbuck, in *A Spell in the Wild* (Two Roads, 2020), a book organised month by month, from September to September, writes about gathering. 'Most people grow out of it: I haven't. My pockets are always full. Leaves and twigs and little bright stones, berries and chips of sea glass.' She is keen to emphasise that these mementoes can store up light and warmth for the colder, darker times. Her poet's prose appreciates the raggle-taggle weeds that are natural to urban spaces, the unbeautiful beauty of pizza boxes and seagulls. 'We work with plastic, with processed water, with air miles, with deforestation and communal bins that stink all summer with that sweet, cloying rot. Thinking magically is also, always, thinking ecologically, thinking about the great wide world that we inhabit. Everything is always sending messages.'

The gatherer, holding the threads of imagination and memory that link human to habitat, nonetheless appears as a solitary, if not lonely, figure. An abiding image from *A Spell in the Wild* is of a private living room with a discreet altar on which some objects change seasonally, some stay the same. The reader can feel the impulses that create the assemblage, and the dirty or delicate textures and processes that go into the preparation of the items as gifts. Small (a pair of hands) and large (the whole world) are brought close. The sense of connexion across a changing scale intensifies in the absence of co-operators, or coven, or congregation. Whatever it is that happens in corporate worship or concerts, when you 'put your hand up in the air', or 'raise the power', when you circulate the fire or offer the sign of peace, is absent. Nonetheless, in Alice Tarbuck's workings, it does not appear that fellowship has been shredded away. The filaments webbing the individual to the environment quiver in their fine, full, tensile strength and extent.

It is attractive to argue for the equivalence of the items that are gathered: the 'natural' is not better, purer, more magical. Some objects do not have a more real presence than others. They are not special for their qualities (or not so much), but mostly because of how they are in or to or of the landscape. Tarbuck is a genius at bringing home to us these things' equivalence in their coexistence, in her and our appreciation, by her intention. I do and do not agree. The intrinsic properties of, say, aluminium foil, how it persists or degrades, the history of its making, seem to me to matter. I want to stop and differentiate them from the properties of stone, its resonance, its erosion. Nowadays it is difficult to do this with things. Tarbuck's ecopoetics of inclusivity can extend to people. My ecopoetics cannot and must not dwell on differentiation in a way that might extend to people. Too many 'nature writers' unconsciously serve ethnofascist assumptions, even when they consciously do not promote them.

Edinburgh remains in Tier 2 and I continue to live in something like pandemic isolation. Another recent book that reflects and companions aloneness is Holly Pester's *Comic Timing* (Granta, 2021). At the winter launch via Zoom, Pester spoke of a poetics of abortivity. The narrator is in the process of undergoing a medical abortion. Meantime, what passes for ordinary life continues externally. At the time, in conversation with Pester, I suggested recontextualising this in terms of a poetics of precarity. The narrator feels 'treated' (what a sinister pun) when she sneaks a rest with a ready meal in the AirBnB property that she cleans for pay. She welcomes, and cooks for, the guests at her housemate's party, without knowing any of them. Accommodation is rented. Another class of people looms out of sight: the landlords, the doctors.

In the long poem that gives the collection its name, the lyrical 'I' aborts itself whenever it begins to speak, in spurts like a stream of consciousness subject to littering and re-routing. The 'I' inhabits precarity; it cannot develop in or be delivered from any environment promising nourishment over time. Looking again at Holly Pester's dramatic pages, I see a poetics of connexion and shredding. In the beginning, 'Act I' offers eight lines of a prose poem that cannot be a monologue or a dialogue, but rather the co-speaking and co-breathing of a self with both self and other embryonically within it.

> shall I shrink in the water or spin (*ah*) here is love and here is death
> (*eh*) it is fare in brine (*ah*) shall I breathe it (*ah*) shall I drink (*ah*)

Broken-off acts of will – 'shall I' – are interspersed with globules of breathing.

Poetry, like song and prayer, connects us with its flow not only when we are the midst of its delivery, overwhelmed, but when we recall it in fragments. A cleaner singing the first line of 'Some Enchanted Evening' with variations at each step of her task is singing the meaning of the whole song. Who knows what scenes my sword-bearing great-grandfather reciting 'The Assyrian came down like a wolf on the fold', his main piece of English, was remembering? Then there was my grasping for a phrase that would calm me in what I expected would be my last moments when a car hit me as I crossed the road, twenty-seven years ago; I found myself thinking, 'Into Thy hands I commend my spirit'.

It is supposed to be otherwise with names, or languages. We are meant to seek correct pronunciations, or to find it significant when we experience loss. There was the Indo-Trinidadian employee in Disneyworld, Florida, who accepted being renamed 'Sweeney'. He seemed to be happy in his job. Names, travelling from mouth to mouth, are shared things of fragmentation. Claudine Toutoungi's poem 'Amendment', in *Two Tongues* (Carcanet, 2020), is amused and in control about the misspellings of her name, which after all appears as author on the cover. Like a music hall spate of nonsense, 'Amendment' riffs over five and a half lines of absurdities: 'Tangerini. Tchoo-Tchoo-tcherini. Tallahassee.' The conclusion is a smart slap: 'And furthermore she's not as foreign as she sounds'. Contrast Christian Campbell's 'Iguana', in *Running the Dusk* (Peepal Tree, 2012). Campbell's poem – both meditation and riposte – begins,

> My friend from Guyana
> was asked in Philadelphia
> if she was from "Iguana."

His language circles through iguana lore and indigenous and Hispanicized Caribbean placenames: Inagua, Heneagua, Wai Ana, Moruga, Hewanorra. The prompt is the questioner's ignorance (another iguana word), and it is answered with ever more serious absurdity, till we are all from the 'land of Iguana'. A frenetic silencing happens in the last couplet:

> And all the iguanas scurry away from me.
> And all the iguanas are dying.

Comic timing indeed, in Campbell as in Pester. Such murmurings accompany at least one reader on half-hidden walks through Edinburgh, the city of many names: Auld Reekie, Embra, Edina, Edo, a poetics of connexions and shredding for tattered, cautiously hopeful times.

Chimes at Midnight

PETER SCUPHAM

For Ann and Anthony Thwaite

Mr Gudgeon, the elderly bookshop assistant in Brian Aldiss's first novel, *The Brightfount Diaries*, is given to sardonic aphorisms: 'A miscellaneous collection of objects is man's only defence against time,' is one I particularly like. Navigating the steps and curlicues of The Mill House at Low Tharston, the Thwaites' home for some fifty years, moving into the long low living room lit with a chequered light from the riverside windows, is to move into a room which is a metaphor for lives lived as travellers in space and time. A Roman bust shares its gaze with the staring eyes and flowing beards of Bellarmines, those stoneware drinking jugs of the sixteenth and seventeenth centuries. (We only wish we could have introduced him to his admired Robin Hildyard, of the Victoria and Albert, whose Exhibition Catalogue of stoneware was delightfully called *Browne Muggs*. Robin had also mentioned Anthony in an academic article, which delighted him.) Books, of course, are everywhere, shelved and nid-nodding to each other, heaped in piles; drawers open to reveal fragments of pottery: '*Sherds, Peter, sherds, not shards.*' This a world of suggestions, shadows of lost knowledge; it exemplifies Anthony's favourite book of Geoffrey Grigson's, *Looking and Finding*, ostensibly for young collectors. We came from a collecting generation of schoolboys: mine were seashells, military badges, wildflowers... Ever since, as a boy, Anthony was given a silver denarius, he had been a looker and finder, alert for the secret signs which lie buried all around us. Both of us shared the National Service experience, jesting that Anthony's acting rank as an Educational Corps sergeant was flimsier than mine, as a substantive corporal, my stripes inalienable, removeable only by a court-martial. But Anthony had refused a commission, so that he could be posted to Libya as a sergeant, where Leptis Magna and civilisation lay baulked and buried in sand. Such rooms as the one Margaret and I are now sitting in, if only in imagination, drinking Red Bush tea and nibbling teacakes, seem to me evocative of the 1950s and a house I knew where pre-Columbian pottery, garage-bills, African textiles and children's drawings all lived in hugger-mugger. In such houses, there was and still is, no sense of display, no angled lighting saying '*Look at me, I'm valuable*', just stuff, loved and used and wonderful.

How difficult it is to remember the conversations, so lively at the time, until they all flew off into the air and the light. Though Anthony's literary antennae were alert to the who's in, who's out, the court news, that was never the staple of our talk. We were more likely to be sharing our interests in minor poets, James Reeves, Clere Parsons, Norman Nicholson... or remembered episodes such as Anthony's return from Virginia by Aircraft Carrier on D. Day. Margaret, who had dramatised *The House in Paris* for the BBC, could be chatting to Ann about Elizabeth Bowen, the book illustrations of Harold Jones – Ann had an original hanging in a shady corner – or the children's books of M.E. Atkinson. Ann, had, of course used the house as a children's lending library well before we knew her, and was having fun recently over a re-issue of her biography of A.A. Milne to coincide with the film. Both Ann and Anthony had a deep sympathy with the Victorian world – *Victorian Voices* is one of Anthony's books I have a special fondness for, and he had published a selection of Longfellow, not quite so quixotic a choice as my friend Patric Dickinson's selection of Newbolt, but hardly a cutting-edge choice of poet. And any stray mention of a name would send Anthony upstairs to reappear triumphantly with the author in question, however minor. I managed to delight him by finding him a set of Miles's *Poets and Poetry of The Century*, that huge conspectus of Victorian poetry, and also for Ann the Moxon Tennyson, with its pre-Raphaelite wood engravings. One of my first thoughts when I think of The Mill House, is of Ann and Anthony's generosity of spirit; the two biographies of Ann's I most admire are her studies of Emily Tennyson, rescuing her from her image as a sickly shadow in Tennyson's life, and Philip Gosse, rescuing him from the bad press he was given in Edmund Gosse's *Father and Son*. Books? Once, the back staircase was the back bookcase, books shelved on the treaders, their backs to the risers...

Time to go into the garden. The Mill House has a river frontage onto that meandering waterway, the Tas, and an Oxford punt, pretending it is about be filled with undergraduates in boaters and girls in dirndls is moored just by the house. I will take Anthony's word for it that he never fell in while punting, his response to a silly drawing I made of him clinging to the pole while his four daughters gazed at him from the sliding-away punt. I never saw Anthony punt, but Ann, however, was wielding a nifty pole in her eighties. The Thwaites had planted many trees themselves, and their meadow was embellished by a gypsy caravan which had seen better days and a table-tennis table, though I shall have to give Ann the glory of being the better player. Here Ann and Anthony held their summer jamborees for East Anglian Writers, here their children and grandchildren camped and made merry, here wood was collected for Anthony, as Keeper of the Flame, to build into lovely living room fires over what seemed centuries of ash.

Two of our most vivid memories of Anthony outside his much-loved habitat are dramatic. Well, sort of. Every year Margaret and I have celebrated the end of summer with a Poetry Picnic, which involves feasting, brief readings by a dozen or so poets and various stalls. Last year Anthony, John Mole and I did a rehearsed reading of the wonderful Silence, Shallow and Falstaff scene from *Henry IV*. Our combined age was, I think, 256. We had all heard those chimes at midnight, from different towers and belfries; there wasn't a dry eye in the garden! And at eighty-three, Anthony took to the boards in our local church, when Margaret directed a semi-staged reading of *Murder in the Cathedral*. The incumbent was demoted to one of those scuttling priests, I played Fourth Tempter, Ann Thwaite was in the Chorus and Anthony, as Reginald de Morville, was, at eighty-three, the oldest knight to have ever killed an archbishop.

Anthony was a charmer, elegant in black with startlingly vivid socks knitted by our mutual friend, Leonie Woolhouse, gardener and painter; conscious of his looks he once murmured that, with Yeats he *'had pretty plumage once'* though when I was one of the judges, who, years and years ago gave Hugo Williams the Faber prize for being the best young poet under forty, said: *'Don't you mean the most handsome young poet under forty?'* *'Both,'* I answered. But I would also like to remember the serious, steady Anthony, the committed Anglican who made no parade of his beliefs but tried to live them. I think of us entertaining Kevin Gardner, a great admirer of Anthony's work, who came over from Baylor to launch his anthology *Building Jerusalem: Elegies on Parish Churches* (2016), when all four of us and Kevin did some Norfolk church-crawling and pubbing – and Anthony and I had a childish mock competition to see which of us had the more poems in the book. Of course, like most old poets, Anthony could feel washed up by the remorseless tide of new writers, and neglected. That comes with the territory; the only poet of advanced years I have known who did not feel neglected was William Wordsworth, who avoided the sensation by making sure he never neglected himself. And I am sure Anthony's last book, *Going Out* (2015) is his best: humane, wry, questioning and kindly. True chimes at midnight.

A Great Prince: Owen Lowery

24 November 1968 – 14 May 2021

ANTHONY RUDOLF

1–Written after Owen Lowery died

Owen Lowery was British Judo Champion while still at school. Before University, he broke his neck during a demonstration, a fundraiser for an injured Judo player. He was in hospital in Southport for at least two years but lost all movement below his neck and, as a tetraplegic, could continue breathing only with a ventilator motor and tracheotomy. In recent years he lived near Wigan and was a long-time supporter of Liverpool, where he was photographed with Liverpool's manager at Anfield. He obtained a BA at the Open University, an MA in Military History at the University of Chester and an MA and PhD in Writing at the University of Bolton. He gave poetry readings at the London Southbank Centre and around the country. He was the subject of a BBC TV programme. His poems have appeared in significant journals including *PNR* and *Stand*.

His good humour and calm temperament helped make public life and outdoor activities possible, as well as enabling a frame of mind where poems could take shape. As John Donne wrote in another context, he had 'faculties / Which sense may reach and apprehend' and so this 'great prince' escaped his prison through poetry and, closer to Donne's poem, love – the unique love he and his wife Jayne bore for each other. Owen Lowery has 'left the conversation', thirty-four years after his Judo accident. At the time of writing, the cause of death is unknown. He had previously come through many a dangerous moment, including a serious car crash last year. He survived thanks to the extraordinary care and devotion of Jayne, his determination, and his mission: to write extrospective poetry. The poetry is not in the pity, still less in self pity, which was absent in the life and in the work.

There are thousands of poems – including a poem written every day for Jayne – and the number of good ones is remarkable. Close friends helped him select poems for earlier books, including Professor Jon Glover (who supervised his PhD on the poetry of Keith Douglas, which was examined by the leading expert on Douglas, Desmond Graham) and myself. His books include *Rego*

Retold: Poems in Response to Works by Paula Rego. Parallel with his ekphrastic Rego poems are a large number, perhaps hundreds, of short essays on particular paintings. His new book *The Crash Wake Poems,* coming out later this year, has been sorted and edited by Professor John McAuliffe from a much larger manuscript.

More details of his remarkable life are available online.

2–Written before Owen Lowery died.

Owen Lowery moves fast. If you don't want an e-mail reply to your reply ten minutes after sending it, save it in a special folder for a day or two. There have been a thousand email chains (second only to my correspondence with Yves Bonnefoy), mute witnesses to a close personal and editorial relationship. I was a privileged reader of Owen Lowery's early or first drafts for many years. Many were later published unchanged. Lowery, in the extreme circumstances of ventilator-dependency and being wheel-chair bound, moves at at the speed of light. He processes data like genius mathematicians.

Lowery's poems are readily accessible, their flow controlled by a master storyteller. He is serious about his vocation, never self-regarding or academic. Turmoil and chaos are tamed in the hundred twelve-liners that make up two thirds of his 'themed' sequence, *The Crash Wake Poems,* his second such work following a series of ekphrastic poems about the paintings of Paula Rego. This book reflects the experience of a car crash involving him and his wife shortly before the Coronavirus lockdown. Survival in his circumstances required tremendous inner strength and mental resource, and then following such an accident the further challenge of having to 'shield' through lockdown.

He 'does it' by means of 'extrospection', the word Keith Douglas used to describe his own poetry. Douglas survived, and then perished, on a differently intense front line. Lowery's PhD thesis was about extrospection in his own work and that of Douglas. Extrospection requires objectivity towards personal experience, however appalling. Another version of extrospection is 'splitting', which was how the poet and psychiatric social worker Eugene Heimler described the way he survived Auschwitz. In Owen's case the line of poetry is, precisely, the front line, perpetually renewed.

Right-Think, Silence, Shaming, Cancellation

SAM MILNE

I was prompted to write this report following my reading of the editorial in the last issue of *PNR* (March–April 2021). The editorial cogently analyses the encroaching ideology of right-think, silence, shaming and cancellation in Western culture. My attention was particularly drawn to the phrase 'objective correlatives have never seemed so perilously subjective', as this threat had struck me forcibly when reading a recent review of John Berryman's *Selected Letters* by Kamran Javadizadeh in the April 8 issue of the *New York Review of Books.* The article to my mind was merely a platform to accuse Berryman (in writing *The Dream Songs,* the letters themselves are hardly mentioned) of racism. Javadizadeh writes of Berryman's supposed 'racist mimicry', his 'white supremacy', the 'racialized structure' of his poem, 'the anxiety at the heart of whiteness itself', and of 'just how white, and therefore how exclusionary and impoverished, confessional poetry, his own included, ultimately could be'. He castigates Berryman for 'the very idea of a lyric subject, an "I" whose interiority the poem presents', being premised, as he argues, 'on the whiteness of that "I"'. He writes of 'the whiteness of the lyric tradition', 'the whiteness of the lyric subject', ignoring the likes of Langston Hughes, Claude McKay and Derek Walcott, not to mention non-English-speaking poets such as Pierre Faubert, Oswald Durant, Aimé Césaire, René Noyau and Leopold Senghor. (Javadizadeh tells us that Berryman approved of Gottfried Benn's lines, 'We are using our own skin for wallpaper and we cannot win.' In that case, surely, one could argue that Henry is trying to escape his white skin in sympathy with Mr Bones?) As for *The Dream Songs* themselves, Javadizadeh quotes (without comment, as it would seriously undermine his argument) from 'Dream Song 119', 'Shadow & act, shadow & act, / Better get white or you' get whacked, / or keep so-called *black* / & raise new hell'. That seems pretty positive to me! Javadizadeh thinks Berryman's future as a significant poet is threatened by what he calls his 'ground of whiteness', his 'racial politics' and his 'racialisation' of (to precis) 'American poetry's turn to confessionalism'.

I decided to try and defend Berryman in the Letters

Column of the magazine, but heard no word in reply, and the letter never appeared. Of course one doesn't expect one's letters to be accepted by the editors, but on this occasion I felt that I had been excluded somehow, cancelled or shamed, by being silenced myself. I had kept the letter as short as possible by not tackling some of the accusations levelled at Berryman by Mr Javadizadeh, but by concentrating on what the letters (ostensibly under review) could tell us about Berryman's poetic methods in composing *The Dream Songs*. I reproduce the letter here, and will add some comments later:

To the Editors
In his essay-review of John Berryman's *Selected Letters* [*NYRB*, April 8] Kamran Javadizadeh barely touches on the letters themselves, preferring to launch a diatribe against *The Dream Songs* instead. A careful reading of the letters indicates some of the psychology and methods lying behind *The Dream Songs*' composition. On pp.591–2 of the edition the poet provides an exegesis of the first Song (and by implication of the whole sequence), 'that it's about The Fall (as indeed much of the poem openly is)... the 'hid' is from God, for nakedness, 'Huffy' is spiritual pride... the 'departure' is from the Garden, and so on. But as I followed the Song thro', mentally, it seemed *also* to dramatize the birth-trauma... the terrible 'departure' from the womb'. It is possible then to look at the complete sequence in this light, with the assumption that the whole of humanity is cursed by sin and death, no matter their ethnicity. The perplexed, self-contradictory struggle between Henry/Mr Bones reflects the phantasmagoric and hallucinatory (they are the poet's own words in the letters) nature of Berryman's personality. The difference in the poem sequence is that this conflict is dramatised through masks and ventriloquism but in a loving, not prejudiced, manner. Again, the letters are revealing on this point. On p.484, writing to Ralph Ross, Berryman says of his daughter Martha: 'children have *far* more facial expressions than we have: she do:– Napoleonic triumph, the weepy-betrayed statesman, cozy-cozy, cunning, who-the-hell-are-you, shy-shy, drop dead, I'm-thinking-it-over, that-food-was-terrific. We drool and adore'. The emphasis is on empathy, not difference. He makes a similar point in another letter (to Luke Evans) when he quotes from Ezra Pound to demonstrate the latter's capacity for affection: 'A black delicate hand / a white's hand like a ham / pass by, seen under the tent-flap'. (In the same letter, on p.230, he condemns a crit-

ic's use of the word 'n-----s': he puts the word in inverted commas himself.) A poet, like a dramatist, can adopt personae to embody the world's multifariousness. I can see little difference between the suffering persona of Mr Bones and that of Anne Bradstreet in Berryman's 'Homage to Mistress Bradstreet' or that of the youngster in his 'The Song of the Tortured Girl'. Would we label Berryman an anti-feminist in these last two poems? Surely not. In a letter to Florence Campbell dated 19 March 1943 Beryman writes: 'I once read Machiavelli and I have Machiavelli's grandson, Delmore [Schwartz], for model, – a man so devious that now and then in the mere ecstasy of the labyrinth he operates against himself.' Berryman knew he could be criticised for his faults, but like every fine writer he was always at odds with himself. In his book of essays, *The Freedom of the Poet*, he writes of Thomas Hardy's poetry, 'that out of such personal misery [he brought] such brilliant joy'. His poetry, like Hardy's, will endure, as it speaks to the heartbreak, and the complexity, of the human condition.

It would appear, according to Mr Javadizadeh, that Berryman has no business adopting a voice that is not his own. (He ticks Elvis Presley off too, in a sly aside, for appropriating 'the blues' for his own privileged white male voice.) What are we to make of Shakespeare's Othello then, or the African-American voices in the work of Mark Twain?

Javadizadeh's article it seems to me is all about himself, and his own prejudices, rather than a review of the book he has been commissioned to write. He ignores Berryman's views on poets and poetry, the problem of being an editor, his teaching methods, his hatred of propaganda and cliché, his travels, his loves, his literary criticism, his poetic methods, his search for a faith, his family, his self-loathing, and his depression and alcoholism. As Sigmund Neumann, a German sociologist, noted in the 1930s: 'discourse becomes meaningless where one's partner has already decided on his position before the discussion has begun. As a result, the intellectual foundations of liberalism and parliamentarism have been shaken' (quoted in Mark Mazower's book on the history of twentieth-century Europe, *Dark Continent*). Javadizadeh confidently states at the end of his piece that Berryman's poetry will never again take centre-stage in American letters. It certainly won't if right-think, silence, shaming and cancellation are given full rein. Somehow I feel that Berryman will survive his commentators. Most great artists do.

Black Orpheus at Oxford

A Footnote

ANDREW MCNEILLIE

Hoping to have the honour of taking the two year academic course in a British University, offered by the British Council to the candidate selected by His Majesty's Ambassador... I would like to state that I am particularly interested in taking a general course in Literature, along with a complete course of the English language, for a better technical understanding of these studies, and mainly for the purpose of criticism and to be more capable of interpreting the monuments of human culture.

So opened the statement to the British Council of Vinicius de Moraes (preserved in the National Archives at Kew), writing some time in 1938, from Rua das Acacias 31, Gávea, a residential neighbourhood in Rio de Janeiro. At this point, the graduate in Legal and Social Studies and author of two collections of poems – *O Caminho para a Distância* ('Path into the Distance') 1933, and *Forma e Exegese* ('Form and Exegesis') of 1935 – was employed by the Brazilian Ministry of Education and Health as a film censor.

A job in censorship is surely a far cry from anything we might nowadays tend to associate with the author of *Black Orpheus*, the champion of the Brazilian underclass, the lyricist and libidinous love poet *par excellence* of *Bossa Nova*, the notorious alcoholic and Don Juan. But in the 1930s de Moraes was profoundly conservative, his symbolist poetry formal and preoccupied with Catholic mysticism, sexual sin and salvation.

As an undergraduate, he had befriended far-right Catholics and as a poet associated with the anti-modernist 'Generation '45'. The major formal influence on his poetics was the sixteenth-century Portuguese master Luís Vaz de Camoës. Otherwise he rooted himself firmly in the European tradition via the French: Rimbaud, Mallarmé, Claudel.

Like all such hopeful exercises, de Moraes's statement to the British Council looked to tick as many of the obvious boxes as possible. The Shakespeare box is wonderfully overblown:

Being a writer myself, or, rather, wanting more than anything else to be a real writer, I endeavour to direct my best efforts to a thorough understanding and diffusion of the creative spirit of the geniuses who made life more worthwhile by thought and creation. In this particular, I believe that England can claim the greatest genius among them all, the one who placed human dignity higher than any other, William Shakespeare, of the works of whom I would like to have complete vision, more than anything else.

The same can be said for the imperial box, where he writes 'ardently' about the possibility of 'living for two years in an English University, in communion with the choicest of youthful intelligence of the British Empire'. As further support for his cause, he cited his books, his work as a film censor, and the fact that he was an officer in the Reserve of the Brazilian army.

This was in April 1938. De Moraes was twenty-four years old. His important collection *Novos Poemos* appeared that year. 'If I am not exceeding my rights to judge myself favourably,' he concludes, 'I can also include a few athletic activities, in which I indulge in my spare time. I swim fairly well, I know a little about jiu-jitsu. I can ride a horse if [it] is not too vicious. I have done a bit of mountain climbing. I can, with a bit of care, come within an inch of a target with a rifle.'

His application did more than come within an inch of the target. On 27 July 1938, A. J. Sullivan, Secretary to the Students Committee of the [British] Council, wrote formally to inform de Moraes that he'd been awarded 'one of the Council's Scholarships of approximately £500 per annum' to enable him to undertake postgraduate work for two years at Oxford University.

The college to which he was appointed was Magdalen. Early in 2008, a friend native to Rio Janeiro asked me if I knew that I shared an alma mater with the grand *afficionado* of Bossa Nova. I did not. Nor that de Moraes had written some 'Oxford sonnets'. I wrote to the then librarian/archivist at the college, Christine Ferdinand, asking after him. She could find no trace of him in the records. Then, some years later, I was researching in Secret Service files at Kew, and stumbled on a listing of British Council files and by chance discovered one devoted to de Moraes. It contained the 'statement' already referred to, and miscellaneous correspondence, between the British Council and Magdalen, as well as more widely within the university, and beyond to the BBC. How could it be that the college appeared to know nothing about him? He began his studies in October 1938.

The then President of Magdalen, Professor George Stuart Gordon certainly knew of his existence. On 25 March 1939 he wrote to the British Council, to report that de Moraes had come to see him over difficulties he was having with his studies. His command of English was proving not quite up to standard and he was struggling. As was hardly surprising, he found himself especially 'at sea... over Anglo-Saxon and Early English'. Gordon suggested instead that he transfer to a Bachelor of Letters (B. Litt) in Portuguese Language and Literature. The British Council supported the proposal and so that became the plan. It wasn't quite what de Moraes had hoped for but he would still have ample opportunity to improve his English.

The next thing we discover is a letter, dated 30 June 1939, from the BBC to the British Council saying that 'Mr V. de Moraes, of Magdalen College, Oxford, is being considered for a temporary appointment as Latin American Programme Assistant' in the Overseas Department, and requesting a reference. Then the trail begins to go cold, and at the same time to get hotter. On 28 August 1939, someone at the BBC acknowledged a British Council letter addressed to de Moraes, to which it replied that he was away until 11 September, having left for Paris and intending to do go on to Italy.

By 3 September Europe was at war. The British Council were concerned for their man and asked if he would now prefer to return to Brazil, offering support, even were he to decide to stay on at Oxford. But de Moraes had seen the writing on the wall and already made up his mind to go home. On 28 August he had telegrammed Sullivan at the British Council from Lisbon saying: PLEASE SEND 50 POUNDS LISBON PORTUGAL BRAZILIAN EMBASSY. On 12 September a concerned British Council official wrote to the Brazilian Embassy at Lisbon wishing to know de Moraes's whereabouts. De Moraes next sent them a cable on 23 September saying he had received the money and that he was returning to Brazil. LETTER FOLLOWING. He then wrote from Hotel Paris, Estoril, Portugal, on 29 September, acknowledging that he could not now complete his course and expressing his gratitude to the British Council, ending with a postscript: 'I have left a few debts behind, at Oxford, that I had quite forgotten. Please get in touch with my landlady, Miss Mordaunt. There are some three pounds of a telephone bill and two others (doctor and dentist).'

So ended the episode that produced de Moraes's 'Oxford Sonnets'. How interesting the outcome might have been had it been able to run its full course in peaceful circumstances. In 1943 de Moraes was admitted to the Brazilian Diplomatic Service. He remained in their employ until 1969, when he was dismissed for alcoholism.

The turning point in his political orientation dated from 1942 when he joined the American activist Waldo Frank (1889–1967) on some travels in northern Brazil where the social deprivation and hardship shocked de Moraes. The collaboration with Carlos Jobim which gave us the Bossa Nova version of Samba, as found in such classics as 'Chega de Saudade', 'Outra Vez', 'Garota de Ipanema' and 'Insensatez' was some way off, as was de Moraes's play *Orfeu da conceição* (*Orpheus of the Conception*), better known in its 1959 film adaptation *Black Orpheus*. In August 1962 de Moraes gave his first performance as a singer, with Jobim and Astrid Gilberto. Perhaps it is not too late for Magdalen College to celebrate their great alumnus with a sixtieth anniversary of this event, in 2022, virtually or otherwise, with samba dancing in the Deer Park.

The Beautiful Game

GABRIEL JOSIPOVICI

Some of us may be football fans as well as readers of poetry, but it has usually been taken for granted that not much unites the average football fan, who is often perceived as racist and no doubt a supporter of Brexit, and the readers of literature. Yet events that took place in the world of football in April, it seems to me, should lead us to question this apparent truism.

In the middle of April, out of the blue, some of Europe's biggest and richest clubs, including Juventus in Italy, Real Madrid and Barcelona in Spain, Manchester United, Manchester City, Chelsea, Arsenal, Spurs and Liverpool in England, announced that they were breaking away from their national leagues and were going to form their own superleague, playing each other on a weekly basis. Such a move had long been mooted and had been dreaded by the authorities, but in football, everyone knew, money spoke louder than loyalty and these teams, many of them (the English ones in particular) owned by foreign billionaires attempting to appeal to a worldwide TV audience, were, it was feared, likely to win out in any showdown. Yet in the event what happened was as cheering as it was unexpected. In England especially the fans revolted, and Boris Johnson, ever keen to show himself a man of the people, came out publicly to say that he would make sure the breakaway didn't happen, even, if necessary, passing legislation to that effect. Within hours cracks began to appear in the united façade of the projected superleague, as the owners of one English club after another backed down. Though the Spanish and Italian clubs held firm (their ownership structures are slightly different), the breakaway was at an end.

What the debacle has shown is something much more interesting than the greed of the owners of the biggest clubs and their indifference to the fans who pay money at the turnstiles. This we knew already, had known for a long time. The superleague promised endless beautiful games between the best teams with the best players, but the furious and more or less unanimous reactions of fans, footballers past and present, managers (many of them ex-footballers of distinction) and commentators, in Britain at any rate, brought to our attention the fact that sport and especially team-sports such as football, are not essentially about beauty at all but about something else. There may be beautiful goals, beautiful passes, even beautiful tackles, and those who play and even those who only watch will roughly agree on what these are in any match and take particular delight in them, but the game is played and watched for different reasons.

But what reasons? Many said competition, the sense that in a particular match, for example, relegation might be at stake for one team and entry into European competition for the other. Both these outcomes, we all recognise would have financial implications for the clubs involved, but for the fans, it seems to me, this was not the primary consideration, nor even was the recognition that the outcome would affect the teams their clubs would be able to field and those they would be playing the following season, and so the quality of the football. For the ardent followers of the team likely to play in Europe there would no doubt arise the thought of the cities this would give them the chance of visiting, Paris, Barcelona, Rome and so on. But more important was the sense of shame at being relegated or of elation at being promoted.

Yet even here a note of caution is needed. I have heard fans of lesser teams voice the opinion that relegation is something they would favour in certain cases because it would ensure their team engaged in competitive matches throughout the season rather than watching them being thrashed week in week out by vastly superior teams. And this is linked to the often-heard remark by fans that they would rather their team fought hard and lost than played safe and won. This always causes debate among fans and pundits alike. Everyone agrees that Spurs under Mourinho were painful to watch this season because his primary instinct has always been to conserve what you have rather than try to get more. In the last weeks of his stewardship this led not only to football painful to watch but also to ever more frequent defeats coming after a winning lead had been surrendered through this type of approach. But had Mourinho's team been victorious and remained in the top four there would have been many who would have traded unattractive football for victory. By no means all, but many.

Thus competitiveness is certainly a key ingredient in the pleasure we take in football but it seems to be bound up with another quality that would have disappeared had the superleague concept taken off: loyalty. 'My grandfather supported West Ham, as did my father, who took me to games when I was five, and I have in turn taken my sons. I have supported them through thick and thin and it is because of the bad times I have been through that I relish the good times we suddenly have this year under David Moyes.' There is again much to be said for this view, but again it seems both true and not quite enough to account for the appeal of football. After all, everyone who has played any sport at amateur level knows that they have done it and relished it for the moment, while taking part, and not primarily because of the team they played for and in. Of course playing for, say, a school or local club team with a good reputation and doing well with them enhanced the pleasure, but it was not its essence.

So what exactly was it that led to the unanimous sense of outrage at what the imposition of a superleague would have entailed? Competitiveness was part of it; loyalty to one's club another. But we have still not got to the heart of the problem. What is the essential element in football that followers of the sport felt was being betrayed? Is there something that unites the kids in the street kicking an old ball or even a pair of rolled up socks and the superstar millionaires playing on exquisite surfaces we watch on our screens? That unites the parent cheering their child in the park game and the dedicated fan who follows Manchester United even to faraway Azerbaijan?

I think there is, and I think it is what sport has in common with art: you do not participate in or watch it for its beauty, you participate in and watch it *because you have an emotional stake in it*. 'You admire, I love,' Stravinsky said when taken to task over his 'unhistorical' rehandling of Pergolesi in *Pulcinella*. What he implied was that the critic had a purely aesthetic interest in music while for him it was his life blood.

The temptation to aesthetize is always with us. It is among those temptations of the intellect that Wittgenstein was always trying to liberate us from by making us aware of them. Art is not history; it is not a vehicle of ideas – but then why does it draw us? Because it is beautiful. Football is not just about money; it is not just about winning – but then why does it draw us? Because it is beautiful. In both cases the concept of 'the beautiful' is introduced because other explanations seem not quite to fit. But that explanation doesn't quite fit either.

What does it mean to have an emotional stake in a sport? Does it mean that once the rules have been established – those pullovers will mark the goal, the pavements will mark the lateral boundaries – and the game has started, you terribly want to win it? Does it mean you have to follow your team through thick and thin so that when it loses you feel deflated and when it wins you feel elated, when it plays badly and wins you feel not quite satisfied and when it plays badly and loses you want it to learn the lesson and play better and win next time? These are perhaps pure versions of the concept, but I think having a stake is even more basic than that. If I watch a match between two teams in neither of which I have any stake I cannot watch it in a pure spirit of detachment, of aesthetic contemplation. Doing so, I soon grow bored and switch off. But usually it does not take long for me to be rooting for one team rather than the other. Perhaps it is the underdog. Perhaps there is no underdog but I start to get frustrated by the way the most talented player in one team keeps disrupting play by throwing himself to the floor and writhing in agony at the merest touch by an opponent. Perhaps I take a dislike to the way one team's central defender consistently goes for the man rather than the ball. Or on the other hand I may take to the way that small, slight midfielder in one team gradually establishes complete control over the game by his calmness on the ball and by the way he distributes it when he has it. Soon

I cannot bear for him to lose and if his team wins in the end I feel elated while I feel depressed for the rest of the evening if it loses. But I have spent a riveting ninety-five minutes, as good as watching any theatrical or filmic masterpiece: the game has been *meaningful*.

I suppose I could train myself to react in this way between two teams in any superleague. But after a while this would no longer work. It would not work because it would not, essentially, be meaningful for the two teams taking part. I once had the good fortune to see the Harlem Globe-Trotters, those basketball superstars. It was great as a child to see them, but I would not even then have wanted to see them week in week out. And it would be the same with the superleague.

And this helps us to understand how and why we respond to other cultural practices. How we respond to individual books, what they mean to us, will often depend on the circumstances in which we first read them. Wayne Booth, the author of *The Rhetoric of Fiction*, once described the genesis of his interest in literature. He was an ignorant twenty-two-year-old on a submarine during the war. The ship's library consisted of two books, an Agatha Christie and *Tristram Shandy*. He recalled reading the latter during the long hours of boredom but always with the threat that any moment could be his last. He was so overwhelmed by the experience that he vowed there and then that if he got out of the war alive he would devote his life to teaching literature. Years later, an established academic, he assigned *Tristram Shandy* to his class for the following week. Well? he asked them when they re-assembled. I couldn't see what the guy was getting at, said one student. Yeah, I kinda liked it, said another. It was OK, said a third.

For the students, Booth realised, it had been just another week's assignment, just another 'great book' to read. For him it had been – what? Something else. And that is the trouble with 'teaching' literature. It tends to become a version of the superleague, one damned masterpiece after another. The way round this has been, for the past few decades, to inject the sense that it matters by opening up the curriculum to things other than masterpieces and exploring through them issues of feminism, colonialism, social injustice and so on. Another, adopted by the best teachers in the century between the foundation of the modern university study of vernacular literature to the 1970s and '80s was to try and instil into students the sense of a living, breathing entity in even such distant and seemingly 'irrelevant' works as *Piers Plowman*, *Comus* or *The Prelude*. To make them *dangerous* again. Soccer fans would have instinctively understood what was at stake.

Letter from Wales

SAM ADAMS

As a fourteen-year-old, my father was apprenticed to a baker in Gilfach Goch. He was the youngest of three children and his parents clearly saw no point in paying the fees that would have gained him a place in a secondary school in the next valley, like his older brother, who eventually became a coal mining surveyor. Communities need bakers, and perhaps they thought it was a career that would keep him gainfully and safely employed for life, with his own business in due course. His father, my namesake, had been a miner all his life, rising through the ranks from 'hewer', as the census termed those who hacked coal from the seam for a living, to 'overman', with responsibility for oversight of the output and safety of a section of the mine. He was also a Salvationist, with a keenly charitable conscience, and a small-time entrepreneur on the side. He set up an arrangement whereby local customers could obtain furniture and household and fancy goods from Cardiff department stores. I don't know how long my father spent in the bakery apprenticeship; I suspect it was no more than months.

If he had promise in any line, it was engineering, which his parents, sooner or later, sought to encourage. From early childhood, as a wilful explorer of hidden places about the house, I knew that one of the cupboards in the mirror-topped sideboard in what we called 'the front room' contained a hefty six-volume set of books on electrical and mechanical engineering. Surely intended to help my father gain professional qualifications in that line, they were in the same cupboard when we cleared the house after his death, still in pristine condition. He had, I believe, rare gifts as mechanic and electrician, and all his knowledge was gained practically, on the job. He was the head electrician – indeed, the only electrician – of the colliery known as 'The Squint', a role that meant, although he was formally 'days regular', he was on call any hour of the day or night. The family was well accustomed to sleep shattered by hammering on the door in the small hours as he was called to an emergency, perhaps the pumps that cleared the mine of water had broken down, or the coal-cutter. He was not one for reading. At about four o'clock in the afternoon, on normal, quiet days, he sat at the table in his pit clothes to eat his dinner, kept warm in the oven for him, after which he would bathe and, with silver hair slicked back, settle in an easy chair to read the morning paper. In a few minutes he would be fast asleep. I never knew any attention-grabbing headlines or news story to keep him alert and awake.

My father was by no means typical. Many mineworkers in various capacities were avid readers: my father-in-law was one. Many found the energy and made the time to be politically active. And some were writers, preserving moments of calm away from their strenuous, exhausting working life with pick and shovel to take up the pen.

I have written recently about Huw Menai, and in the past referred to the most memorable poetry to come out of the south Wales coalfield, that of Idris Davies, himself a miner and the son of a miner. Thanks to the recommendation of a fellow worker underground, Davies was inspired to write by the radical poetry of Shelley and, given the opportunity occasioned by the loss of a finger at work and the 1926 strike, after which he was unemployable, embarked on a course of self-education that led to him joining the first teacher training intake at Loughborough College and then Nottingham University (1930–32). In the latter institution, D.H. Lawrence, poet, son of a miner, had preceded him a generation before (1906–08).

Chance, like as not reinforced by the strong will of a mother, and determination, were needed to cast a poet, or a writer in any genre, from the mould of a manual labourer. If you want insights into the process and the product you could do worse than find a copy of *These Poor Hands*, the autobiography of B.L. Coombes, first published by Gollancz as a Left Book Club Edition in 1939, in some senses an antidote to Richard Llewellyn's *How Green Was My Valley*, published the same year. Robert Morgan (1921–1994) was another who achieved the remarkable transformation from collier ('hewer') to writer – and artist into the bargain. In the foreword to his autobiography *My Lamp Still Burns* (Gomer, 1981) he writes: 'Some of my boyhood, all my youth and several years of manhood were spent as a coal miner... My father, his father and grandfather had all been coal miners, so it seemed natural that I should become one... I crawled and worked in a seam no more than two feet thick... I have written the following pages to confirm some of the reality and to strengthen my heritage.'

Robert Morgan came from Penrhiwceiber in the Cynon valley, between the Rhondda and Merthyr Vale. Its pits, dating from about the third quarter of the nineteenth century, had begun closing soon after Nationalisation and were all gone by 1984 (a common case), but Robert had quit mining some decades before. Having twice won the short story competition at the South Wales Miners' Eisteddfod, in 1947, at the age of twenty-six, he gained a place at Fircroft College, Birmingham and subsequently trained as a teacher at Bognor Regis College of Education. In 1953 he became a teacher in Hampshire, thereafter devoting his professional life to children with special needs, a calling that requires infinite patience and tact as well as great skill, until he retired in 1980 to give all his time to his creative interests. He had chosen art as his special subject while at Bognor Regis, so that for him, almost always, painting and drawing went hand-in-hand with writing, and had a common subject: the valleys of south Wales and the experience of mining. In his art, the pithead gear, the stack and engine house, and the toppling terraces of steep valley streets, constitute a stark iconography, with the sun glimpsed, through whatever smoke or cloud or haze, the colliers, grateful, rose to from their struggles (and what struggles) in the darkness of the pit. He had several one-man exhibitions, at galleries in Portsmouth, Winchester and Guildford, at the Mermaid Theatre in London and the National Library of Wales. In addition to his autobiography, he published *The Night's Prison* (Hart-Davies, 1967) which includes poems and 'Rainbow Valley', a drama broadcast on BBC radio, and a number of poem pamphlets.

I corresponded with Robert and met him a few times, once I recall when with Roland Mathias we read poems to an audience in Builth Wells. He was a man whose impressive, quiet charm easily held an audience and attracted a host of friends in the literary and creative arts. For all his subsequent experience, going down the pit with his father at the age of fourteen left an indelible mark:

> In the thin seam
> Raw knees were nothing.
> We learnt pain like reading,
> Knew the vocabulary of punishment
> In rhetoric aimed at officials
> And rockbound hovels.
> Nothing was easy,
> Not even walking out
> Two miles to shaft and sun.
> When you faltered free of lamplight
> I remained, copying your style
> With steel-box and hatchet.
> Then I locked the tool-bar for ever
> And took the strain of books.

'Crusoe in England' and de la Mare's *Desert Islands*

JOHN CLEGG

In October 1958, Elizabeth Bishop reviewed Walter de la Mare's anthology for children, *Come Hither*, in *Poetry* (Chicago). It had been first printed in 1923, and just reissued by Knopf after de la Mare's death in 1956. 'Although much of the poetry I admire is not to be found in it, I shall think this is the best anthology I know', Bishop began. (W.H. Auden and Stevie Smith shared her opinion.) 'He loves "little articles", home-made objects whose value increases with age, Robinson Crusoe's lists of his belongings... [...] After the poems come the notes, and the book is well worth buying for them alone. It is a Luna Park of strayed and straying information.'

'Home-made', so close to 'Robinson Crusoe', might naturally remind us of Bishop's 'Crusoe in England': 'Home-made, home-made! But aren't we all?' But it is worth noting that, while 'Robinson Crusoe's lists of his belongings' appear nowhere in *Come Hither* – neither among the poems nor among the compendious notes and additional material – they form the primary subject of a different de la Mare anthology, *Desert Islands* (1930). I think this anthology was a major source, perhaps the major source, for Bishop's poem.

To describe it as an anthology sells *Desert Islands* short; it is, in fact, the text of a lecture delivered to the RSL, on Crusoe, Defoe and desert islands in literature, which takes up 70 pages in large print, followed by 250 pages in small print of 'rambling commentary' – a mix of de la Mare's own notes and commonplace-book, similar to *Come Hither*'s 'Luna Park of strayed and straying information' but even more disproportionate to its main body. There had been US editions from Farrar & Rinehart in 1930 and 1947; it was the sort of book which would naturally have appealed to Bishop.

In a letter to the critic Jerome Mazzaro, Bishop says that when she wrote 'Crusoe in England', she 'hadn't re-read *Robinson Crusoe* for at least twenty years' (letter of 27 April 1978). Here is the same scene, then, in *Robinson Crusoe* itself (which Bishop would have only had vague memories of), 'Crusoe in England', and *Desert Islands*:

Defoe, *Robinson Crusoe*:
> When I took leave of this island, I carried on board for reliques the great goat's-skin-cap I had made, my umbrella, and my parrot.

Bishop, 'Crusoe in England':
> The local museum's asked me to
> leave everything to them:
> the flute, the knife, the shrivelled shoes,
> my shedding goatskin trousers
> (moths have got in the fur),
> the parasol that took me such a time
> remembering the way the ribs should go.

de la Mare, *Desert Islands*:

> So perfectly realizable is its story, that we should be little surprised if on arriving to-morrow morning in [Crusoe's birthplace, York], to find neatly reposing in their glass case in the Town Hall the very reliques and souvenirs which our friend tells us he carried off from his island for sweet remembrance' sake: his hairy hat, his umbrella, and maybe – stuffed, glassy-eyed, a little mothed and dusty - one of his later parrots.

Defoe's is a simple checklist of 'reliques', of which nothing subsequently is heard. De la Mare, like Bishop, has imagined an afterlife for them, presented to the local museum, authentically moth-eaten and decrepit. A few pages later in *Desert Islands*, de la Mare describes how ineptly Defoe handles the death of Friday in the unreadable *Farther Adventures of Robinson Crusoe* (1719); I doubt Bishop had read this continuation (I don't think there was a cheap edition available), and may have taken de la Mare's summary as a hint for the heartbreaking final lines of 'Crusoe in England'.

Here, *Desert Islands* may have given Bishop suggestions for her Crusoe; elsewhere it may have given her suggestions for his island. Here is Bishop again:

> My island seemed to be
> a sort of cloud-dump. All the hemisphere's
> left-over clouds arrived and hung
> above the craters—their parched throats
> were hot to touch.
> Was that why it rained so much?
> And why sometimes the whole place hissed?
> The turtles lumbered by, high-domed,
> hissing like teakettles.
> (And I'd have given years, or taken a few,
> for any sort of kettle, of course.)
> The folds of lava, running out to sea,
> would hiss. I'd turn. And then they'd prove
> to be more turtles.
> The beaches were all lava, variegated,
> black, red, and white, and gray...

And here is de la Mare, retelling at two removes a story from a sailor-turned-New York taxi driver called Christiansen, who had ended up stranded with his crewmates on a Galápagos island around 1906:

> On the twelfth day they sighted land. It was Indefatigable Island. 'Nothing but lava. So there we was.' For months this little band of derelicts managed to keep life in their bodies by drinking turtles' blood [...] Their boat having been turned to tinder, they wandered on over the lava beaches of the island, pining for water and searching for food. Inland, among unapproachable volcanic hills, streamed down a blessed rain from the clouds above.

Defoe's original island is not volcanic, has beaches of sand rather than lava, and (on Crusoe's side at least) has no turtles, apart from one which washes up dead in the tide. The only difference between de la Mare's island and Bishop's is that Bishop has - so much the better for Crusoe - made her volcanic hills, where the rain falls, accessible. A paragraph later, in Christiansen's narration: 'Nights was the worst!' Some lines later, in 'Crusoe in England': 'Dreams were the worst.'

There are further parallels that could be drawn out: de la Mare's notes on archipelagoes, loneliness, and goats, especially, seem to me to answer to lines and passages in 'Crusoe in England'. But there's one further de la Mare link elsewhere in Bishop that I want to draw attention to - much more dubious, and very possibly a coincidence, but in any case showing a link between the two poets' imaginations.

This is the epigraph to *Geography III*, which is really a poem in itself: a found poem, taken from an 1884 geography textbook which Bishop had received as a gift from John Ashbery:

> *What is Geography?*
> A description of the earth's surface.
> *What is the Earth?*
> The planet or body on which we live.
> *What is the shape of the Earth?*
> Round, like a ball.
> *Of what is the Earth's surface composed?*
> Land and water.

And it continues, becoming (as Bishop told Susan Howe) 'rather hysterical' as the questions ramify and spin off from one another.

And here is de la Mare, in *Desert Islands*, straying far from his subject as usual: 'The manual of geography in use at my dame's school was always referred to as the little yaller book. I learned in it that an island is 'a piece of land surrounded by water' [...] And *land*, what of that? Why not make sure of that too? Well, land is 'the solid part of the earth's surface'. And water? Water is a 'colourless, transparent, tasteless, senseless compound of oxygen and hydrogen in liquid state convertible by heat into steam and by cold into ice'.'

Bishop and de la Mare must surely have had different editions, one adapted for the UK and one for the US. But the section of text from which they quote is common to both: Bishop quotes from the sixth and tenth lessons, de la Mare from the third. It is indeed a 'little yaller book'.

Poems and Features

Montpeyroux Sonnets

MARILYN HACKER

Village gone silent in pandemic mode.
School's closed. One small girl with a bike is out.
The narrow street recedes into its doubt
of baker, butcher, neighbour. On the road,
cars rarify, whisk by trees that explode
in redbud, apple blossom, presage fruit.
'Have you had your first, your second shot?'
Masked conversations shrivel into code.
When I was here last, I could walk three miles
back to my histories in Arboras,
sweater in backpack, if the wind turned cold.
I could see people's faces. Chatter was
about elections, new café, roof-tiles.
When I was here last, I was not so old.

When I was here last, I was not an old
wolf enclosed all winter in a cave,
no pack, no steppes, no prey, who didn't starve
except for conversation. I unfold
memories like a blanket, stained with mould,
out of some cupboard. Today, I can save
what I'll remember, click my phone. I have
a hundred shots, almost two years I hold
in my palm. On a rooftop , garden shed
clutter, heat, noon, all stun me to be still.
A worker's laugh below scratches the silence.
Two languages, two books, stay shut, while in-
stead of reading, I let sunlight fill
the question/answer blanks inside my head.

The question/answer blanks inside my head –
numb feet, blood pressure – get in the way of care,

joy, generosity. I am a bore.
Age is a bore. Thinking of it's a dead-
end street, huis-clos, a tertiary road
that stops out in the middle of nowhere
at a mound of dirt, under a bare-
bone-blue sky, tyre-tracked. It might have led
out to the mountains, to a different town
where people, unmasked and miraculous,
eat and drink, talk to strangers face to face.
Twilight estranges a familiar place.
Grey clouds look bloodstained as the sun goes down
on autochthons, on refugees, on us.

On autochthons, on refugees, on who-
ever averts her eyes from sun and dust
in the glare of nearly noon, a bus
spatters pebbles passing, one of two
that stop here daily. Within the blue
noon light, everything pauses, bikes, upthrust
iris spears, the bakery, the post
office. The desultory interview
two bored old men conduct goes on, laconic
questions/answers unchanged in a decade.
It's an excuse to speak, rendezvous made
behind masks now, grudgingly, still, a choice
to be incensed, jocular, ironic ,
to have a face, have memories, a voice.

To have a face, have memories, a voice,
lowered in conversation over wine
or coffee, in a semi-public place.
To stop in Uniqlo because that jean-

jacket would fill a non-existent space
in the closet. To take the bus. To take the train....
but I did, fled Paris, builders. The only noise
my mind's contagious clangour, its refrain
repetitive. No sandblasting. No drills,
only the fretting and the self-reproach,
which has a name, depression, and seeps back
despite late-morning sunlight on the hills
whose ovine clouds recede as we approach,
driving to Friday market in Gignac.

We drive to Friday market in Gignac
in Julie's car, recuperating years
of spring and summer villages, house-shares:
two beds, one kitchen, somebody's notebook
out on the terrace. It's my turn to cook
dinner... Now is now. The omnipresent wears
us down, but market plenitude still cheers
us up. Strawberry season. While I pick
up two punnets, Julie chooses blettes

– and they'd be delicious with cabillaud.
Apricots, almonds, ginger, and should we get
a poulet rôti anyway? As if it were
the same. Everyone's masked. Laden, we go
back through the cobbled side streets to the car.

Back down the cobbled side streets to the car,
a week later, under cold spring rain,
with blettes, fresh tuna, strawberries again,
and not a lot to say. Perhaps we are
fraying at the edges of a year
where nothing but uncertainty was certain.
Only my fight or flight nerves were alert in
the market square, its plenitude, its cheer
diminished, masked. Don't handle fruit. Don't chat
with the girl selling fromages de brebis
or the fishmonger. Thinking separate thoughts, we rode
past mountain vistas looking oddly flat,
past vineyards, to the empty streets of the
village gone silent in pandemic mode.

A Week in Gdańsk

SINÉAD MORRISSEY

Inside St Mary's Church in Gdańsk stands a Clock of Everything. At fourteen metres, it was the tallest clock ever built when Hans Düringer completed it in 1470, and it remains the largest wooden astronomical clock in the world. So beautiful its creator was allegedly blinded upon finishing it, the clock is the first thing that greets you as you enter the basilica by the north transept, its dark medieval wood highlighted by the white walls. Composed of three discreet but interlocking sections, like the Trinity, it functions as an at-a-glance answer machine, the Google of the fifteenth century. Of course it tells you the minute and the hour. But if you want to know the phase of the moon, or the relation of the moon to Taurus, or the relation of the sun to Capricorn, or the relation of the sun and moon to each other, it will tell you that too. And at noon each day, beneath the forked tree of our Fall, like hatches to the realm of metaphor, tiny doors open and out wheel the three Kings followed by the four Evangelists followed by the twelve Apostles followed by Death brandishing a scythe – an order which undermines the hopeful face of Mary with her baby enshrined at the clock's base as, Christ notwithstanding, Death's caper reminds us, Time does for us in the end.

It's the last week of August 2020. In a late-summer window of grace from the ravages of Covid-19, I've trav-elled here to accept the European Poet of Freedom Award for my collection *On Balance,* translated into Polish by Magdalena Heydel. Apart from having to wear a face mask in the hotel corridor, things seem pretty relaxed. Shops, cafés and museums are all open. The quayside is crammed. Along the Long Market, street hawkers tout luminous balloons. Any foreknowledge I have of Gdańsk is over seventy years old and in the wrong language: the sing-shattering sentences of Günter Grass's maniacal *Tin Drum* unspooling in my head.

I've only been here an hour when I walk into St Mary's. After contemplating the Clock of Everything (or as much of it as I can within a span of ten minutes), I begin to explore. An exhibition of black-and-white photographs flanks the southern side of the nave. I step closer to discover Pope John Paul II on board a makeshift chapel built as a ship surrounded by Soviet-era tower blocks. He's gesturing out towards a sea of insects – ants or locusts descended on crops, something swarming. Except – they're *people.* Men. Women. Children. A million Tri-City citizens turned out to welcome their native son. I stare. It's a hot June day in 1987. Back home in Ireland, they are yet to uncover the mass grave containing 155 corpses on the grounds of a Magdalen Laundry run by the Sisters of Our Lady of Charity in Dublin, or the remains of just under 800 children at the Bon Secours Mother and Baby Home in Tuam. The Catholic Church sex abuse scandal is brewing while this Pope will dither and wring his hands. But for the crowds on a disused airstrip in Zaspa, he's a light in the darkness of Communist dictatorship. Flip the context, switch the frame, and an alternative meaning emerges, the two truths not cancelling each other out but co-existing – rival languages in the one city – and I don't know what to do with my revulsion. It doesn't go away, but is added to, and unresolved. It pulses in the air in a shaft of sunlight like the shimmering, throughother aura of migraine.

That first evening, as the sun slides into the Baltic, I walk past the clattery restaurants, the replica *Black Pearl* with its useless paraphernalia of seafaring, the ship museum named after the Stakhanovite shock worker Sołdek, solid in its own shadow, out past the bridges and the fairgrounds and the glass apartment blocks of the New Poland to what's left of the Lenin Shipyard. I know shockingly little about Solidarity. I know what Lech Wałęsa looks like. From a dimly recalled News broadcast in the early 1980s, I know he made a speech into a hand-held microphone surrounded by a crowd of badly dressed men. It's all post-industrial ruin now, this city-inside-a-city that once housed bars and cinemas, leisure complexes and an on-site hospital, where 20,000 workers built over 1,000 ships for the navies of Poland, Bulgaria, Yugoslavia, East Germany, the USSR. It reminds me of Belfast before the multi-million, Titanic-inspired facelift of its own derelict shipyards. It reminds me of afternoons spent wandering among overgrown cobbles and haunted graving docks, rainbow oil in the puddles, abandoned vessels sinking deeper into their own rot and a ravening sky overhead I loved as much as I did because it couldn't care less.

The Lenin Shipyard is in-between destinies. The old industrial order has collapsed. The Gdańsk municipal authorities are applying for this crucible of revolution to be designated a UNESCO World Heritage site, which would see it partially restored and partially redeveloped, but for now artist co-operatives have moved into its windy spaces, reclaiming its radical heritage for themselves. The bricks of a drawing office are still blackened, the glass so smeared or smashed it admits no possible interior, but a Pride flag juts out of an upstairs window – and this in a country where local authorities have campaigned for the establishment of 'LGBT-Ideology-Free Zones' (comprising up to one third of Polish territory) under the homophobic rule of Law and Justice. Among scrubland further off, a crimson Alexander Lukashenko descends into hell, decapitated Belarussian citizens strewn round him as his *publicum.* On a gangrenous slipway, steampunk junk figures made out of typewriters, springs, radiators, lamps, fans are either emerging from the waters or stalking back into them – you can't tell which way they face without faces – the anthropomorphised essence of mechanical über-production that's been the story of this site for a century. Or our future, once production lines have ceased altogether, when a handful of survivors will make do with what's to hand: a raggle-taggle army keeping alive the dream of what being human means.

The horror of a human being that is *The Tin Drum*'s Oskar Matzerath witnesses the start of World War II in Danzig/Gdańsk when SS soldiers attack the Polish Post Office where his biological father Jan Bronski works. True to actual events, Bronski and his colleagues hold out for fifteen hours against impossible odds, until Jan is betrayed by Oskar for a toy drum and shot by the Nazis as an illegal combatant. The Polish Post Office building is still operational and contains, in a ground-floor corner, a three-room exhibition space in honour of its defence. Like a museum of a museum, exhibits from the 1930s – a telephone, a desk, a telegraph machine – invite our dumb appraisal while typed white cards on the walls explain patiently what they mean. But there is the SS Attack Plan, salvaged from who knows where after 1945, all seven meticulous pages of it, detailing exactly how the building is to be stormed and exactly what is to be done to its occupants, including the caretaker, his wife and their eleven-year-old daughter. And along two walls, degraded objects from the mass grave the Polish postal workers tumbled into after being executed by firing squad on the 5 October 1939: a nit comb, a shoe, a watch, a miraculous medal.

My visit coincides with the fortieth anniversary of the signing of the Gdańsk Agreement between Lech Wałęsa and the Polish Communist authorities on 31 August 1980 which granted Solidarity the right to exist as an independent Trade Union. I don't know what any of this means but on Sunday 30 August I make my way to The European Solidarity Centre: a discombobulating architectural marvel boasting gardens on the roof and trees and rusted gantries within the galleries, a building 'like the inside of somebody's head' as a friend put it when I sent him a photograph. It's immediately obvious from the museum's stature that this is the site of pilgrimage, the immortalisation of a particularly precious socio-political, quasi-religious narrative of which I know next to nothing, and as I enter the resounding atrium and buy a ticket, the idea begins to take hold that I somehow missed *the* story of the Cold War. Not because the Cold War wasn't important – in my family the Cold War rang its extirpating nuclear alarm *all the time* – but because the story of Solidarity simply transpired on the wrong side of the line.

More powerful than the 95 theses nailed to the door of All Saints' Church in Wittenberg, in that they didn't split a world in two, but eventually dismantled it entirely, the 21 demands of the Interfactory Strike Committee hang proudly spotlit in a dark hall. Handwritten across two plywood boards used by workers for marking out templates, these had been mounted onto the shipyard's iconic Gate 2 on 18 August 1980, as sympathy strikes ignited across the country and official news channels reported Anything But – Honecker's tank manoeuvres, a Polish-Czech trade conference in Prague, a rally of the Young Communist League. The first three demands are the most famous, and rightfully so, because combined they undid the Soviet mono-bloc from within:

1. Acceptance of free trade unions independent of the Communist Party and of enterprises, in accordance with convention No. 87 of the International Labour

Organization concerning the right to form free trade unions;

2. A guarantee of the right to strike and of the security of strikers;

3. Compliance with the constitutional guarantee of freedom of speech, the press and publication, including freedom for independent publishers, and the availability of the mass media to representatives of all faiths.

Read on and the demands become more parochial, more worker-orientated, more tethered to their particular time and place, though the strain of unfettered idealism remains: a day of rest on Saturdays; an increase in the commuter's allowance to 100 *złoty;* paid maternity leave for three years. It is a document of vast discrepancies of locus and scale, the product of all-night sessions of the Inter-factory Strike Committee held in the shipyard's canteens and meeting halls, of speeches and debates fuelled by weak tea, apples, bread, whatever an impoverished populace left at the gates – a say-everything-now document because the chances of it actually being listened to or acted upon are so minuscule you may as well. But it was also brilliant, in that it weaponised the shibboleths of the governing structure, citing ILO articles on free association and Trade Union rights which the Polish Communist Government had itself ratified in 1957. Solidarity, among many other – profoundly contradictory – things, was the ghost in the machine of Communism, which spoke its language and wore its clothes. Give into it, and everything unravels. But don't give into it, and the gap between doctrine and reality which the governing authorities ignored becomes unbearably exposed, and everything unravels anyway. For the Communist authorities in Poland, Solidarity was Catch 22 from the start.

There was talk, apparently, Deputy Mayor Alan Aleksandrowitcz tells me later in the week over lunch, of a military helicopter flying low and simply strafing the strikers from the air. Or of a gunship. Which would not have been inconceivable; which would not have been without precedent. You don't have to think of East Germany in '53, Hungary in '56, or Prague in '68: Poles rose up in 1970, and again in 1976, and were shot for their trouble. And they were *young.* A wall of detainee mugshots from 1970 reproduced courtesy of the Institute of National Remembrance resembles a high school yearbook. A granular black-and-white photograph shows the body of 18-year-old Zbigniew Godlewski carried through the streets of Gdynia by his peers; beside it the bulletpierced jacket of 20-year-old shipyard worker Ludwig Piernicki, housed behind glass like a relic or the Turin Shroud.

I don't know any of this. I don't know the name Edward Gierek. I don't know about the economic masterplan that crippled the country as debts incurred by gargantuan foreign borrowing were eventually recalled. I don't know that the logo of Solidarity – *Solidarność* – is all squished up on purpose, giving itself a hug. But as I watch footage of the negotiations and signing, Wałęsa brandishing the tackiest pen in Christendom (as long as a baton and as thick as cigar, John Paul's anodyne smile encased in plastic), Deputy Premier Mieczysław Jagielski, officious, thin, clinging for dear life to the wrong side of history, I believe I know this packed hall on film after all. I believe I know the quality of late summer sunlight falling though its windows and its order of business. I believe I know its smell.

In Poland, the *form* of a long-atrophied Revolution was reinvigorated, lit up from within, to be deployed against itself. And whilst the static political ideology of my family – the ideology of Western Communism loyal to the Soviet Union – practically guaranteed that the *content* of Solidarity, what it actually meant and threatened, more or less passed me by, I still recognise the form. The film of the signing still tumbles me back, deftly as Proust's madeleine, to Transport House in Belfast on one of a million interminable afternoons, waiting for my parents to finally stop talking and take me home. There are the same trestle tables. There are the same overstuffed ashtrays. There is the same shuffling of papers and the same rudimentary sound system, microphones spiked on tables like attendant crows. My stolen Saturday grinds on. I sit on a chair, daydreaming, or read heretical Enid Blyton. My parents ignore me. Even when the speeches are over, they're still stuck in a die-hard cluster at the front, my father holding forth with extravagant hand gestures, cutting a Trot-leaning enemy to shreds, jutting his head, while a conference organiser folds banners into boxes and a cleaner arrives to pick up the teacups and sweep the floor. With his stocky build and horseshoe moustache, Wałęsa reminds me of any number of the men I knew who, like my parents, existed in the Venn diagram intersection between the Transport and General Workers' Union and the Communist Party, and I have the weird idea, suddenly, that if I put my hand inside Lech Walesa's pocket, I'd know what I'd find: a handkerchief, a pipe, matches, random coins.

My Communist grandfather hated Solidarity, not only because it was fuelled by the Catholic Church and the CIA, not only because its Western advocates included Ronald Reagan and the British National Party, but because it was matter-out-of-place. Why stage a Revolution against the Revolution? But what twins they were, I think, my grandfather and Lech, what brothers they might have been, as I watch the unlikely victor borne out on his comrades' shoulders to address the ecstatic crowd. A memoriam poster of my grandfather captures him shouting into a megaphone in *agitprop* colours, king of his own (admittedly far smaller) moment, and I play it out in my head, this shared penchant for rhetoric from high places, as the two of them scrabble upwards, Lech onto the roof of a shipyard trolley in Gdańsk, my grandfather onto a barricade in Belfast, to raise their arms and speechify. *The great only appear great to us because we are on our knees – let us rise!* said James Connolly said Jim Larkin said my grandfather, over and over through my childhood, at TUC conferences or May Day rallies, standing tall, taking aim, David against Goliath, his barrage of abstract nouns the slingshot that would bring injustice down.

In Belfast, during the wildfire days of August 1969, my grandfather scrambled up on an electricity transformer box and urged Turf Lodge residents to dig up the road. Bombay Street was a smoking ruin, thousands of Catholics had fled their homes and B-Specials in Shorland armoured vehicles with Browning machine guns mounted on top were on their way. *What shall we dig with?* shouted a man in all innocence, like Johnny to Eliza in the bucket song, missing the point. *Dig with your fingernails!* How could my grandfather have resisted the high-octane rush of this other wildfire August, had he lived here instead of there, a mere eleven years later? How could the man who hi-jacked a bus, robbed a bakery and distributed free loaves to mothers and children during the Ulster Workers' Council Strike of 1974 possibly have resisted Solidarity's righteous call?

For here they come, the ordinary people of Gdańsk, bathed in beneficent sunshine, also bearing bread – though now it's both the bread of basic sustenance and the body of Christ, as Gate 2 grows adorned with wreaths of rosaries, flowers, Catholic iconography. The generosity of Gdańsk residents was pointedly extravagant. They gave more than they had. With shops picked clean and hunger marches, such extravagance involved ingenuity and privation as well as kindness; their faces shine with the thrill of upstanding transgression, the elation of risk. For the sin of achieving Jagielski's signature to Solidarity's demands, retribution is naturally coming – though not by air, sea or Soviet tank. In sixteen months, on 13 December 1981, First Secretary of the Polish United Workers' Party and founder of the Military Council for National Salvation General Wojciech Jaruzelski will undertake Brezhnev's dirty work for him by imposing Martial Law. Poland's own tanks will roll in. On the first day of military rule, the Moscow Cinema in Warsaw will screen Francis Ford Coppola's *Apocalypse Now* and photographer Chris Niedenthal will immortalise the gesture: a stone lion, wires, trees, snow, a green tank parked on a white street with soldiers gesticulating – the end of the world.

Martial Law lasted until 22 July 1983. Three weeks later, my mother visited Poland on a Communist Party holiday. She hated it. The buildings in Warsaw were pockmarked with bullet holes. In the hotel bedrooms, prostitutes lay in wait for male delegates while men in trench coats hung round street corners selling black market pornography. Vegetarian at the time, she was served a hairbrush bristle jutting out of a mound of tinned carrots. I have since wondered why my mother didn't return to Belfast and tear up her Party Card. Wandering through the European Solidarity Centre, I now wonder if anyone mentioned Martial Law, if any of the immediate context of internment camps and curfews, murdered protestors and censorship was part of her travel brief. I ask her later. It wasn't. In the traumatised, volatile atmosphere of Martial Law's aftermath, perhaps the blithe arrival of privileged Western Communists was not a particularly welcome phenomenon. Perhaps there was more to the hairbrush bristle than she thought.

There is much to commemorate in Gdańsk this week. On 31 August, the actual anniversary of the Agreement, Magdalena Heydel and I accept our joint award. Knowing more about the rationale behind the prize, of the contours of what was achieved here forty years earlier,

the honour is weighty and sharp. Gdańsk Mayor Aleksandra Dulkiewicz introduces the event. She's a busy woman. Earlier that afternoon, she presided over a celebration of Solidarity at the Monument to the Fallen Shipyard Workers – three towering anchors-cum-crosses nailed to the sky – and is on her way to a rally in support of the Belarussian uprising unfolding as she speaks. Afterwards, she will stay up into the early hours of September 1 to mark the beginning of World War II when, hours before the assault on the Polish Post Office, German forces in the shape of SMS *Schleswig-Holstein* attacked Westerplatte, a Polish military outpost ten kilometres along the coast.

Drastic bifurcation is the tenor of the day. At the Monument to the Fallen Shipyard Workers, *two* Solidarity celebrations take place: the Gdańsk Municipal Authority ceremony and the Law and Justice ceremony, *and each so different, on either side of a wall,* explains Barbara Frydrych, Director of the Mayoral Office of Culture, *it is difficult to understand how they could be paying tribute to the same movement.* During the War commemoration, Law and Justice take over altogether, refusing to allow Mayor Aleksandra Dulkiewicz her pre-agreed role. For if Solidarity was many – profoundly contradictory – things, it split like mercury in 1989 when the Goliath it pitted itself against eventually toppled. And a substantial part of its core, with the gleeful sanction of the Free Market and the blessing of the Vatican, rolled right.

Nazi plans for the storming of the Post Office involved 150 soldiers and lightning attacks from multiple directions to preclude successful defence. The storming of Poland's nascent post-Communist democracy by Law and Justice has been equally brutal and multi-directional: control the media, control the judiciary, 'other' a marginal group. For now, the most 'othered' Poles are members of the LGBTQ+ community, though as all good children of Socialists know from Martin Niemöller's Lutheran Confession – *First they came for the Communists, and I did not speak up because I was not a Communist* – the category of public enemy under fascism is inherently unstable and expansive. Every few days, Ana Matusevic of the Gdańsk Cultural Institute sticks a rainbow to the front door of the office and every few days it's taken down. For the ceremony I wear a badge combining the Solidarity victory sign with the colours of Pride, a badge which attests to Solidarity's diametrically opposite legacy: the little-voiced standing up against a socio-political monolith that would deny their right to exist. Which is a simple thing to do. Which is *something.* But when a woman approaches me afterwards to thank me for wearing it, and then asks if she and her girlfriend should leave Poland, I am ashamed to the roots of my hair of the easy privilege of my position. Lives are now at stake here every day in ways I will never be able to fully appreciate. I wonder how long it would take for democratic institutions back home to realign into something more akin to Law and Justice's iron teeth – ten years? Five? Perhaps less than one might hope; perhaps less than one might think.

The Free City of Danzig, created as part of the ratification of the Treaty of Versailles on the 15 November 1920 and in existence until its annexation to the Third

Reich in 1939, is the improbable country into which Oskar Matzerath is born in 1924, with complete adult consciousness and gifted with hyperthymesia – the capacity to never forget. In the chapter 'Long-Distance Song Effects from the Stockturm', Oskar climbs the Goal Tower, pitches his 100-decibel voice across at the neighbouring City Theatre and shatters its windows one by one. Because it's clever and secret and safe and elaborately destructive and because he can. That this action is a metaphorical prefiguring of *Kristallnacht* is obvious. For all that Oskar's stunted figure is an anathema to the Nazis, who keep sending his 'presumptive father' Alfred Matzerath the paperwork that would allow his deviant son to be 'eugenically exterminated', Oskar still functions as the symbolic spirit of National Socialism, drumming his insouciant *I-want* mantra through the novel's catalogue of atrocity, an Angel of Death in short trousers dispatching as he goes. Towards the end of my week in Gdańsk I pass under the restored City Gate at the east end of the Long Market and emerge onto a square. *There* is the tower, *there* is the theatre, and I find I can trace precisely how Oskar took aim and sang, in the jittery days on the eve of war, just before a Jewish toy seller vanishes and a horse's head is hauled out of the Baltic crawling with eels and Oskar's mother commits suicide gorging on fish and a fragile city state – as idealistically forged as the Weimar Republic and as riven with compromise – begs to be smashed.

And where smithereens of Oskar's vandalised glass would have showered down, I come across a plaque. *In Memory of Paweł Adamowicz Mayor of Gdańsk 1998-2019.* And so I learn that this is in fact the spot where, on the 13 January 2019, twenty-seven-year-old Stefan Wilmont, recently released from prison, climbed up on a temporary stage during the city's biggest annual charity event and stabbed Paweł Adamowicz three times before parading around, delighted, with the knife in his raised right hand. Because he was angry. Because it was elaborately destructive. Because he could. The next day the fifty-three-year-old Mayor died of his injuries. In 2017 Adamovicz, pro-immigrant, pro-European and an advocate for LGBTQ+ rights, had been named on a 'public death certificate' issued by the far-right All-Polish Youth.

Poland is not yet lost insists the National Anthem, composed in Italy in 1797 two years after the Third Partition had wiped out the Polish-Lithuanian Commonwealth. Wilmont may have been mentally unbalanced, but the unmitigated torrent of hate speech on Law and Justice-controlled state television to which he was exposed in prison was a factor in his behaviour with ramifications for us all. *Poland is not yet lost so long as we shall live.* In the aftermath of Adamovicz's assassination,

under the banner Stop Hatred, thousands marched in silent candlelit vigils across the country, reclaiming a more charitable Poland for themselves. Adamovicz's last words – *Gdańsk is generous Gdańsk shares its good Gdańsk wants to be a city of Solidarity* – are inscribed on the plaque as a fitting memorial to the man who had said of growing up amidst the bitter dislocations of the Soviet era: *we hardly saw a place for ourselves in this double world.*

Such attics cleared of me! Such absences! I unfold my city map for the umpteenth time and spot oddly designated 'non-cemeteries': discreet squares named for what once was but is no longer; a nominal signification of grief. Many of these turn out to be German places of rest or *Friedhöfe* (from the Middle German 'peace huts'), levelled post-1945 after the German-speaking population had fled West in advance of the Red Army or been forcibly expatriated. But there are other resonant absences. The Cemetery of Lost Cemeteries memorialises a total of twenty-seven destroyed graveyards and a necropolis. It openly honours the Holocaust Disappeared by citing Polish-born German Jewish poet Mascha Kaléko, whose books were burned by the Nazis in 1933, as part of its central inscription: 'For Those Without a Name'.

The Cemetery of Lost Cemeteries acknowledges and venerates the complexity of the region's heritage. As Law and Justice exert control over Poland's historical narrative by means of swingeing simplification, itself an act of violence – criminalising any public statement of Polish complicity in the Holocaust, for example – the Cemetery of Lost Cemeteries utters a quiet political counterstatement. With its interplay of Christian and Judaic design, presence and absence, shadow and light, it is a space which, rather like the Clock of Everything, appears to open endlessly outwards, including all the city dead in its tribute: German, Pole, Jew, anyone otherwise othered, anyone in between. On my final morning, I visit the Historical Museum (free on Thursdays) and find myself in the Hall of Great Council, or Red Room. Above my head *The Apotheosis of Gdańsk* by Isaac van den Blocke, an Anabaptist from a family of Dutch craftsmen who had arrived in the city in the sixteenth century, fleeing persecution, unfurls its audacious vision in grandiloquent oils. And this too opens outwards, for here are cities within cities, gates within gates, a garden giving endlessly into the distance like an infinity mirror. I stand beneath it for a long time. And because the pillared entry to the Kingdom is framed in a rainbow and because God's blessing on the city is inscribed in Hebrew, I photograph it and send it to my father, who has never been to Gdańsk. I want to let him know how precious such luminous multifacetedness has been.

Broom, or The Flower of the Desert
Stanza 2
BEVERLEY BIE BRAHIC

from Giacomo Leopardi, *Canti*, translated by Beverley Bie Brahic

And men loved darkness rather than light.
  —John 3:19

Look here and see yourself mirrored,
Vain and foolish century,
That forsaking the road
Of thought's resurgence,
Turn your back on it
And boasting of this, call it progress.
All the geniuses whose misfortune
It is to have had you as father
Go singing your praises, though
Left to themselves, as often
They deride you. Don't count on me
To go to my grave covered in such shame;
But rather the disdain of you
That I hold close within my heart
I'll have shown as openly as I can,
Even if I know that oblivion
Is the prize of those who fail
To please their contemporaries.
So far, I've laughed at my fate
Which you are going to share.
You go dreaming of liberty
And would again shackle thought,
Thought that alone has raised us
In part from barbarity, that alone
Increases civility, that alone
Helps to advance the common good.
So the truth about the harsh fate
And lowly place nature assigns us
Displeases you. And therefore you
Like cowards turn your back
On reason's light, and call those
Who follow it vile; and great souls
Only those who, deluding themselves, or others
Astute or fools, exalt
The human condition even above the stars.

Smuts and Shrooms

LISA KELLY

In Search of Cowbane Rust

Daughter, Son, some rusts are rare
Their hosts are rare, that's why
If I'm long gone, don't despair
I'm on the Broads with watchful eye

Their hosts are rare, that's why
I paddle down Wheatfen dyke
I'm on the Broads with watchful eye
Slipping off with otter and pike

I paddle down Wheatfen dyke
Checking for cowbane at the edge

Slipping off with otter and pike
Fingers brushing willow and sedge

Checking for cowbane at the edge
I found clumps, but none had rust
Fingers brushing willow and sedge
Hope of a parasite come to dust

I found clumps, but none had rust
If I'm long gone, don't despair
Hope of a parasite come to dust
Daughter, Son, some rusts are rare

Red Data List of Threatened British Fungi: Mainly Smuts

Smut, lie down with me in annual meadow grass that tickles
our pelts. Smut, be barley covered and reeking of beer,
a bearberry redleaf prim on each pinkish part. Smut, with your bedstraw hair,
bestow no interloper a bird's eye view. My promise, a primrose
with its fairy caretaker that no bog asphodel, no bone-breaker
will I brook, smut. As a chick weeds out a worm, I will weed out
all burrowing doubts, all jealousies, all winter green looks
on our love, smut, which would shrivel us, smut. Smut, be not false.
This oat-grass ring, I twine about your finger, smut.
Think of me when a foxtail, smut, lifts to expose a gland,
stinking of March violets, to deceive you, smut.
They'd have you frogbit, smut, back in the pond where you
were spawned, mounted and belly grasped. Glaucus sedge creeps
in damp ditches, smut. Weep for such green hell bore away
with earth's daughter, smut. Loose your hair. See how sedge flowers in spikelets,
smut, and love always pricks. Lie down with me in meadow grass that tickles
our pelts. Revel in mudwort, smut. I could call you close to Limosella, smut,
cloaked in tiny white stars, a northern bilberry redleaf prim on each pinkish part.
Passion marks us, smut, with a purple small-reed stripe, smut.
My rare spring sedge, smut, tender as fresh shoots.
My reed canary-grass, smut, sensitive to noxious airs. Saxifrage smut,
I cannot help but repeat saxifrage smut, the brassy instrument of you played.
Sing of prickly yuletide, sea holly smut. They are small spored
with their white beaks, sedge smut, poking and prodding and stinking, smut.
They are not sweet – they confuse carnal with vernal, smut.
Damn the white beak-sedge, smut, worn by quacks as if we were plague, smut,
with their aromatic herbs, smut. What rare pathogens we are, smut.
What gall smut, to detest our dark teliospores. Yellow toadflax
on them all, the cowards that croak. Yellow toadflax on them all, smut.

Mushroom to Svamp

How fungi transform material, we admire
as Google, from English to Swedish,
translates mushroom into svamp.

A beautiful word, a swamp-cum-vamp,
a siren emerging from a quagmire
to appeal to our fetishistic death wish.

Alice in IKEAland swallows SVAMP
regurgitates a lamp. We may desire
a frosted orange agaric, but our outlandish

dream is out of stock. Alice has SVAMPIG,
a grey/white sponge, the soft side, a dish-
cloth, the coarse side for stains that require

more vigorous cleaning. SVAMPIG
commands, *Wet before use.* No PISH-
SALVER, *Drink me,* but she aspires

not to shrink, nor whirl in the gyre –
O Thanatos, into Swedish
you translate. Spongy is SVAMPIG.

Mushroom Machine

1. The urge to begin with 'I'
Must be resisted. This default mode
Close to the manufacturer's setting
Most users would probably choose.
Brain at wakeful rest, daydreaming
About which lock 'I' fits
To start the whole engine churning.

2. Alan Turing is on the new £50 note.
His nephew says he should be remembered,
Not primarily for code breaking, but for
Asking, 'Can machines think?'
Our smartphones can write plausible poetry.
The Computer's First Christmas Card
Does not begin *iwishyou.*

3. Professor Adamatzy inserted electrodes
in oyster mushrooms and held a flame
to the cap of one. Other fruiting bodies
responded in the mycelial network
with a sharp electrical spike –
potential for fungal computers
and mycelium as environmental sensors.

4. Time of year: autumn; adjective: electric;
Two singular nouns, not normally
In the same sentence: mushroom, machine;
Another adjective: pale; verb: signals.
Electric autumn
An oyster mushroom signals
*Beyond the machine**

* *Poem Generator: Create a Haiku in Seconds*

Scarlett Caterpillar Club

Who begot the gap must gawp at the gape
between species crossed

What sort of society are you?
Sounds like one I'd wish to join –
vivid, kind of cute, definitely can-do
with undulating segments and all those implied legs.

I look you up for entry requirements:
Are you a fan of the great outdoors?
You might enjoy grasslands or woodlands.
Looking for a change – willing to metamorphose?

Yes, that's me, an Emperor Moth caterpillar.
I'm up for selection; to be sprinkled with special spores.
Just the lucky few, mind. We get to settle down
in sexy soil or luxurious leaflitter. Begin to pupate.

O, to be in an exclusive club. The thought of it
turns your insides to mush, causes your head to explode
with a bright orange fungus. Club motto:
Need it like a hole in the head.

Alternate Reality

Because sometimes there are bits of ourselves we just can't deal with.
Coping mechanisms are exhausted.
Dead inside sort of describes it –
everything is too much effort and we crave
feelings, aliveness, call it fecundity. The hospitalised
guy who injected himself with psilocybin,
his name withheld, could be any one of us,
imposters in the great game of surviving ups and downs,
just hanging on, and when Polly puts the
kettle on, why not make it a brew worth the risk of kidney failure,
liver failure. Surely,
magic comes with risk and boiling down shrooms into a mushroom tea, after
noting the potential therapeutic effects of hallucinogens in
online research is understandable, relatable.
Psychoactive effects from psilocybin could be a miracle cure, but the
question is, how we do things –
recreationally or destructively.
Shrooms leading to multisystem organ failure, fungus growing in your blood,
treatment in intensive care, and a prescription of long-term antifungal drugs is
ugly and unexpected despite any compensating
vivid flashbacks, or in medical terms, hallucinogenic-induced persisting deception disorder.
What are we going to do with reality?
Xtc, etc. is illegal, but taking the edge off with a natural high –
you have at least thought about it haven't you? The relief of reaching an alternate
zone of being.

On Charlotte Mew

REBECCA WATTS & JULIA COPUS

Rebecca Watts talks to Julia Copus, whose biography *This Rare Spirit:
A Life of Charlotte Mew* was released by Faber in April. Copus is also the
editor of *Charlotte Mew: Selected Poetry and Prose* (Faber, 2019).

WATTS: I'd like to start with first encounters, because one of the things that perplexes me about Mew is how limited her reception has been over the past century. It was only a few years ago that I found her poem 'The Trees Are Down', somewhere near the beginning of an anthology of 'modern verse' I'd borrowed from the library, and was blown away by its freshness – that unique quality Mew has of channelling emotion and complex moral convictions into rhythms that are both speech-like and intensely musical. And I remember thinking: why haven't I heard of this poet before? But then struggling to find other examples of her work.

COPUS: For a long time, I was only vaguely aware of Charlotte Mew as a name in poetry. We certainly never came across her work in school, for instance. Then in 2005, Deryn Rees-Jones brought out an anthology called *Modern Women Poets*. It covered a century of women's poetry in English, and as Mew was born exactly one hundred years before me, it happened that I was one of the last poets in that book and she was the first. The title of her opening poem there – actually her most famous poem, 'The Farmer's Bride' – gives the impression of something well-mannered and bucolic, but the poem itself is neither of those things. It was accompanied by two other extraordinary pieces, 'Rooms' and 'The Trees are Down', and between them this trio made a deep impression on me. There's something about that unusual synthesis you sum up so well that lends the poems their particular power – the way in which she captures what you might call the speech of the heart in these agile, elastic rhythms, in lines that are sometimes sprawling, occasionally clipped and insistent, but always, as you say, musical. She once wrote to a friend that although she believed emotion was 'the first requirement of poetry', it couldn't be communicated without proper technique, which, she said, could only 'be got with work and patience'.

W: Speaking of which, when did you realise she was going to become a major focus for your work?

C: I initially had the idea of doing something quite short. I first got in touch with Matthew Hollis at Faber back in the spring of 2013, about the idea of including Mew in their *Poet-to-Poet* series – pocket-size paperbacks of past poets selected and introduced by contemporary poets. He told me the series was currently dormant but was enthusiastic about the idea of Mew in general. We spoke on the phone and I can't remember whether the first thought for a longer book came from him or me, but I see that I emailed him a few months after that initial

conversation to say that 'I do, in spite of everything, feel really drawn to doing a book on Mew' and 'I can't seem to stop myself digging and getting excited about her'. Famous last words!

W: We'll return to the digging in a moment, but while we're on the poems I want to ask you about that distinctive formal technique of Mew's. In your introduction to the *Selected Poetry and Prose* you note the difficulty of reproducing the impact created by Mew's unusually long lines, pointing out that 'the indentations of the overturned lines combine with Mew's own indentations to result in what looks like a deliberate patterning that was never intended by the poet'. Certainly when you look at a poem like 'Madeleine in Church' (Mew's longest by far, at 222 lines), its shape – determined by that miraculous syntax, which accommodates a dramatic combination of stream-of-consciousness reflection, theological argument, raw emotion and concrete observation – is at once striking and baffling, and difficult to apprehend within the confines of the narrow page. I've often wondered whether these formatting difficulties are one of the reasons Mew's originality has been overlooked, historically – because they make her poems appear, in print, to be much more conventional creatures than they actually are. Was there any discussion in the course of putting this edition together of honouring Mew's original insistence that the long lines in her debut collection *The Farmer's Bride* should be preserved intact? Did the formatting create a headache for you at proof stage, as it did for Mew back in 1916?

C: Yes! There was discussion. It took place in the summer of 2019, at a time when my mother was seriously ill in hospital, and I was also trying to work on getting the biography finished. The stress of all that somehow added to my sense of urgency, my desire to speak up on Mew's behalf – because, as you say, she had complained to her own publisher about this very issue. She believed the full force of her lines would be diminished if they were broken up, and because of her insistence, the original book was brought out in a wider shape than normal – what her publishers called 'a rather ugly quarto page'. Anyway, the upshot was that my powers of persuasion weren't as strong as Mew's! The editorial team were sympathetic and did what they could: a smaller font was used and the page margins narrowed to try to accommodate the long lines. But I still wasn't happy, and after I'd seen the proofs – so quite late in the day – I asked if there was any possibility of using the wider ('short royal') format that Faber sometimes uses, but apparently the additional width still wouldn't have been enough to allow all the lines to remain unbroken.

My concern wasn't about wanting to clarify where a new line began (Mew's capitalisation at the start of lines takes care of that) but wanting to avoid altering the *look* of the poems. Mew's lines can vary wildly and suddenly in length, but she also uses a wide variety of indentations, meaning any new indentations that the publisher introduces can throw a poem completely out of shape. Short of bringing out a bespoke edition, there just didn't seem to be a perfect solution. I think what we ended up with works for the most part. But that's a great point you make about how the visual standardising – or taming – of Mew's wayward lines in more recent editions of the work may have caused readers to overlook the originality of her poetry. At any rate, it was certainly noticed in her day. The American critic Louis Untermeyer, who was a big fan of Mew's work, once signed off a letter to her with 'Strength to you – and your large & flexible line'.

W: And more strength to her absolute command of drama and pathos in 'The Farmer's Bride', which blasts open the very question of why and how the eponymous woman might be expected to be tamed. You mention Mew's 'insistence' – her technical conviction and her confidence in adhering to her artistic judgements – which is certainly a quality that comes through in many of the letters you cite in *This Rare Spirit*. Yet at the same time Mew was a notoriously private person, fearful of the exposure inherent in publication and the impact this might have on her life and her family. I'm interested in what Mew's reticence has meant for you as her editor and biographer.

C: As her biographer, it made me feel quite uneasy for a while about digging into the darker corners of her family's life and revealing some of the very details that she'd put so much energy into keeping secret. Writing about them did feel intrusive at times; on the other hand, there is no question that she wanted her work to be known, and my hope is that the biography will send people back to her work. But in practical terms the reticence wasn't too much of a problem. Of course I would have loved to discover reams of diary-type notes in Mew's hand, but even without that, there was a fair amount of source material to draw from. I had some lucky finds while researching the book: I tracked down the privately owned diary of one of her cousins, for instance, and found the medical records of her brother in a local history centre, letters and artefacts in private ownership, a couple of previously unpublished poems and stories and so on. Interestingly, Mew's poem 'Fame' expresses a deep ambivalence about the idea of being publicly known: on the one hand, the newly famous speaker longs for the 'heavenly places' of her old, more private, life, but on the other, she's not sure she could turn her back on fame now that she's had a taste of it: 'Yet, to leave Fame, still with such eyes and that bright hair!' If these are Mew's own thoughts on the matter, it's a very self-knowing and honest response – and, I expect, not an uncommon one.

W: Unearthing new original material must have been hugely exciting, particularly in the context of Mew's relatively small published oeuvre. How did you track down these primary sources? Were you guided by the existing secondary literature (previous editions of Mew's work, for example), or were you largely starting from scratch?

C: In 1981, Carcanet brought out a major edition of Mew's work: *Collected Poems and Prose*, edited by Val Warner. Val told me that Michael Schmidt had initially pointed her towards a collection of Mew's manuscripts in the British Library; she'd then traced an unpublished 1960 PhD thesis by an American scholar, Mary Davidow, in which she found half a dozen uncollected poems, a story and the titles and sources of other prose works. When I first came to Mew, I was hugely grateful for both these texts, but especially Val's book, because the essays and stories had never been collected before. Val died last year, under sad circumstances, and I feel lucky to have spoken with her just a few months before that happened. We had a long phone call in which she wished me luck with the biography.

The finds I made myself generally came from other leads. For instance, I discovered a previously uncollected story in an 1897 edition of *The Woman At Home* which I'd bought from eBay! The material from private collections came to light gradually and in fits and starts, through tracing descendants of Mew's friends and relatives via genealogy websites. I also amassed copies of a large number of letters to and from Mew, most of which are scattered through archives in the States, and I was given a huge head start in this by Giselle Falkenberg whose mother Betty had been collecting the letters for a planned book on Mew when she died. Giselle sent me what she had and I was able to build on that. Her generosity was typical of the sort of reactions I had from people while working on *This Rare Spirit*.

W: Your method and meticulous attention to detail radiates from every sentence. When you place us in the room or on the street beside Mew, the scene is always underscored by your close observation of documentary evidence: architectural plans, meteorological records, magazine advertisements, images from *The Illustrated London News*... As someone who's worked a lot with archival and manuscript collections I was amazed at the range of sources you consulted, and the skill with which you piece the disparate facts together to construct such a vivid and illuminating narrative, explicitly resisting the urge to speculate at every turn. A less determined biographer would surely have baulked at the scale of the undertaking.

C: I'd say two things motivated me in this approach. The first was inexperience – in other words, fear! As a first-time biographer, I had to begin by feeling my way forward, one step at a time. From the start, I knew I wanted to provide a sense of atmosphere and context – the weather on a certain day in Bloomsbury, or the interior of a restaurant Mew dined in, for instance. I found it annoying if I didn't know some of these details so I turned to whatever I could to try to uncover them. The other motivator was that I'd read Penelope Fitzgerald's *Charlotte Mew and her Friends* (published in 1984), and though I'd enjoyed it as a reader, when I started on my own book I found myself growing more and more frustrated with it. I couldn't find any proof for some of the events presented there; for others, the timing was wrong; names and relationships didn't match with the evidence I'd collected, and so on. It unsettled me because I knew that some of our basic sources (letters quoted in Mary Davidow's thesis, for instance) were the same. But the notes section in Fitzgerald's book is slim and many of the quotations are unreferenced, so it was impossible to check her assertions. The conclusion I reached was that Fitzgerald had made certain decisions about Mew's character and life story before writing the book, and had then arranged the narrative around those key ideas. She once told the French newspaper *Libération* that she had an interest in 'people who seem to have been born defeated or, even, profoundly lost', and one of the main themes in her book on Mew is that Mew was a frustrated lesbian, on the receiving end of repeated rejections. Following that idea, she outlines Mew's unrequited love for three specific women – but one episode spins on a misquotation from a letter, and others aren't referenced at all.

In a sense it's a problem of presentation – the fact that Fitzgerald's book is presented as straight biography. Of course, all biography involves interpretation, and no biographer can hope to get to the absolute 'truth' of a life (even if such a thing existed). We can only tell the story as we find it. That was advice I heard from another biographer and it became a guiding principle while I was writing *This Rare Spirit*. But in the course of my research, I came across a letter from the daughter of one of Mew's close friends, Edith Chick, which reveals that many of the details in Fitzgerald concerning the Chick family were 'fantastically wrong'. She says in the letter: 'The trouble is that if the only facts one knows about are incorrect, it raises doubts about the more important ones.' In view of all this, I felt a certain burden of responsibility – to be as scrupulous as I could with the verifiable facts, and to provide details of sources for my readers. My initial intention hadn't been to write an account that differed in any significant way from Fitzgerald's, but simply to place more focus on Mew's writing – to offer a poet's insight, if you like, into some of the points of contact between Mew's life and work. But the more inaccuracies I discovered, the more it worried me that a person from recent history might be so quickly misrepresented – especially as some of the inaccuracies have been repeated; the danger is that they start to harden and take on the patina of fact.

W: It's fascinating to think there might be fundamental differences in how a fiction writer and a poet do biography. I also found Fitzgerald's book very readable, and I think that's mainly due to its rendering of Mew as a character, as in a fiction – someone who participates in set pieces of action or drama through which they reveal their 'true' character as envisioned by the writer. In this sense it seems Fitzgerald's aim was to create the version of Mew with the most symbolic potential.

C: Yes, I think you're probably right. Mew made a comment in one of her letters that intrigued me, about the natural patterning that occurs in our lives: she said that 'Life has an odd way of falling with patterns even for untidy people & more for the others who lend it a hand'. Whether or not that's true, further shaping is clearly necessary to make a book readable, as you suggest; and in order to shape, you have to reflect on the life as a whole and look for patterns that point to character traits – repeated occurrences, behaviours and reactions, for instance. But I think to envision the character too early on in the writing process, or too rigidly, is to risk closing yourself off from some of the nuances of the real person – some of the things you might otherwise discover about them. There's also the temptation to set people in situations that didn't happen, or that didn't happen in quite the way you describe, in order to fit your narrative. For instance, Fitzgerald has Mew's sister, Freda, break down 'beyond recall' in the early 1890s with symptoms of schizophrenia and claims that her father, Fred, 'asserted himself for almost the last time' by insisting she be sent from London to his native Isle of Wight. In reality, Freda was only pre- and early teens at the start of the '90s. Her medical records reveal that she didn't start showing signs of schizophrenia until she was nineteen, and by that time Fred had died and wasn't around to send her to the Isle of Wight or anywhere else. The first version might make a good story – but whose story is it?

W: This liberal approach couldn't be more different from the attentive narrative perspective of *This Rare Spirit*, where we essentially observe Mew – sometimes from a distance, when the evidence is scant, and sometimes very intimately – as she moves through life and tries to succeed on her particular terms as a writer. Can you say a little more about how your experience as a poet inflected your assessment of those points of contact between Mew's life and work?

C: One of the things I mean by 'poet's insight' is simply that, as poets, we know what it's like to sit with a poem and go through the redrafting process, a process that's often demanding and can be exasperating – revising lines, trying to marry sound to sense; that sinking feeling that comes with realising you have the wrong word, the sort of desperate hopefulness of searching for a better one, and the joy (if we're lucky) of finding it. There's a passage in *This Rare Spirit* where I try to reconstruct Mew doing this with her poem 'Smile, Death' – a scene I built up from a close look at her drafts of the poem. The other thing is that I'm aware that the way my own life feeds into some of my poems isn't always straightforward. Some of the most seemingly impersonal poetry might in fact be freighted with personal experience: for instance, I wrote a poem about the Hero and Leander myth which is informed by (and only exists because of) a fraught, rainy night on which I waited for a person to visit me when my marriage was breaking down. There appears to be a similar interplay between Mew's lived experience and some of her poems: there are many details that parallel details from her life. We also know Mew believed other poets' character traits could be discerned in their work. In an essay on Emily Brontë, she argues that 'the true – the one original likeness – Emily herself has sketched: it is outlined in these slim pages of neglected verse', and she picks out particular traits by quoting them from the poems: the 'quenchless will', the 'savage heart', and the 'resentful mood', for instance. For some poets (and no doubt other writers too) a tight web is built between the life and the work, and the web might in some sense support the life – even, at times, enable it. I think Mew was one of these writers.

W: I love that essay on Emily Brontë – not just because it exemplifies the impassioned, lyrical heights Mew achieves in her best prose, but also for its lucid expression of her unassuageable belief in the power of literature to manifest and to liberate the human spirit. What do you think your readers stand to gain from engaging (or indeed reacquainting themselves) with Mew today?

C: Mew's poems questioned several of the orthodox assumptions of her day – concerning, for instance, the treatment of the mentally ill, the balance of power within marriage, and the unswerving wisdom of an all-seeing deity. Many of her themes remain powerfully relevant today. In challenging how things stand, her writing generates a degree of uncertainty but also holds within it the possibility of change for the good. It teaches us compassion for people who are 'other' than ourselves, and it shows us how much can be learned from paying closer attention to the natural world: 'the larks that cannot praise us, knowing nothing of what we do, / And the divine, wise trees that do not care', as she puts it in one poem. Perhaps most relevant of all in these globally uncertain times, her poems suggest that something like equanimity can be restored by listening in on the stillness that lies just outside the chaos and noise of human life. 'Everything there is to hear,' she tells us, 'in the heart of hidden things'. I hope *This Rare Spirit* gives readers a window onto how the work was produced and shaped – by a particular life, mind and time – as well as a sense of the sacrifices that were made in order to produce that work. There are always risks inherent in choosing to be a writer – perhaps especially a writer of poetry, and perhaps especially (even now) a female writer. Writing biography forces you to think hard about how we measure the worth of a life, and looking back on Mew's life and work – the extraordinary courage she showed – it's difficult not to feel inspired by her example.

'Berries' and other poems

LINDA ZISQUIT

Not Now

Nabokov said language
has many forms of
quiet kindness, refusals
of stark alternatives:

never can mean *not always*
and *impossible*
may mean *not now.*
How many times have I

opened a letter in search
of the hopeful word
and found only its shadow,
its empty promise.

And yet I keep reading
the lines to find
another possibility
in the very syllable

already spoken,
the one that closes
the heart only to
wedge it back open.

Her Beauty

It wasn't that, a premeditated act. Or even a glimpse
of Eden. She was the one I admired, her beauty
I desired. As he taught me the gears

and how to smoothly shift upward or down,
we navigated a mountain
of swift and transient passage.

It was the day I learned to drive a stick-shift car.
We met at their house. As I walked past her
holding a dishcloth over her delicate arm

I smiled as if not knowing where our ride in the hills
would take us. Does she remember that moment
outside the kitchen door when her terrified eyes met mine?

Why did I think I could have it both ways?
Desiring her thin silk blouse with its geometric design,
her shining face when she tried it on

and how I could not bear to not be her inside it.
Who would think I'd be the one to dazzle him,
standing in the same room with her?

Sappho admires the man who sits
next to the woman she loves. And he
becomes in that instant a god

her beloved must love instead of her.
But I was taken by her beauty
as later by my own in the arms of her beloved.

There are times I think I see her
coming towards me on the street
but no! it's an old woman, lips tight,

whiskery eyebrows raised in disbelief
that I am free to walk the same earth.
Or it's a young girl about to begin singing.

Berries, or What to Save and What to Discard

We belong as much to the things we throw
away as to the things we keep
—Hilton Als

I mean the text
buried and one day found
in a dusty box
labeled 'On Dry Land'.

'Disaster,' he said.

Was it a disaster?

those barberry twisted lines
spilling their purple nectar,

enticing the stunned reader –

like birds in Minnesota
dashing into windows
and falling dead
against the soft ground
after drinking from the early ripened
berries of the juniper.

Amazed viewers
who always thought the flight of birds
an elegant sweep
suddenly look up to see
a bloody brawl –

A god it must be!
A Dionysian pleasure god
whose grapes ferment
in one day

like the grapes of Noah –

after months and months
in a sealed craft

never mating
or touching flesh –

the feeder thinks of nothing but feeding:

day animals by day
night animals by night.

It was all he could do
to lie down alone on dry land
and catch his breath

to plant a tiny stalk and weep.

It's not the first time
mounds of Bohemian waxwings
are found with their berry-stained beaks
dead on manicured lawns at dawn
victims of neither vultures
nor foolish men
but like their relatives

the cedar waxwings
with a genetic tendency

to indulge on the fruit
of the juniper or crabapple
before flying south
whenever a first frost
comes early
and the red berries
beckon
with their plump curves.

After a few hours
their drunkenness subsides
if they survive
the early bite.

Was it a disaster?

those barberry twisted lines
that were meant to untangle
the truth.

Why not destroy the evidence,
tear it to shreds
so forgetting will be a place
to begin?

The ancients said, use word-play
try scrambling the syllables
till only the victim
can decipher a meaning
and forgive.

Or place the words in seawater
till the letters blur.

Or throw down the tablets
and shatter the failure.

This is not a sober branch
or even a twig
or leaf
or vein of chlorophyll.
Not a seed.

How can they speak of the only good man
left on earth
who takes his wife and children
and doesn't plead
for anyone else
to be saved?

A blameless man follows the path
laid out for him
by the gods.

And *always, always*
the heart is submerged
in the word 'sorry'.

Sudden Ascent

Arseny Tarkovsky & Peter Oram

BORIS DRALYUK & IRINA MASHINSKI

In the English-speaking world, the major Russian poet Arseny Tarkovsky is known, if he is known at all, as something of a bit player in the work of his far more famous son, the filmmaker Andrei Tarkovsky. Fans of the son's *Mirror* (1975) and *Stalker* (1979) will have heard the father's poems, piecing together their meaning from the subtitles, but are unlikely to have sought out better translations; and even if they had, they were unlikely to find translations as instantly enchanting, as subtle yet energetic as those gathered here.

It may be more surprising to learn, however, that a great many Russian readers also encountered Tarkovsky's poetic voice before they were able to read his poems. The experience of Irina Mashinski, a Russian-American poet born in Moscow in the late 1950s, helps elucidate the peculiar role Tarkovsky played in Russian literature – that of a messenger from the past who, miraculously, not only survived but remained whole, untarnished, eternally fresh.

*

One time, in early spring, in one of the upper classes of secondary school, when dying of boredom during a lecture on literature, I reached over to the shelf that ran along the classroom wall and pulled down the first book my hand chanced upon – a blue-backed selection of works by the 18th-century Turkmen poet Magymguly Pyragy. I remember the warm page, brightly lit by the school-day sun, and the striking poems – not at all exotic, though 'eastern', masterfully built yet at the same time alive. This sensation came and went: the pages would cool down then light up again. Taking a look at the table of contents, I discovered that all the living versions belonged to Arseny Tarkovsky. The name, which sounded beautiful in Russian, was new to me, although by that time I was already a fairly experienced reader of poetry. It is somehow natural that my first meeting with a poet destined to become one of my favourites was not a meeting with his poems, but with his translations. The next one – this time real – happened thanks to his son's semi-prohibited films, Mirror *and, a little later,* Stalker, *which my friends and I went to see somewhere in the Moscow suburbs. Then, unexpectedly, an LP was released – a recording of Tarkovsky reading his poems. And so it happened that Tarkovsky came to me and to many members of my generation as a voice and as an image, and only later through his books.*

The charm of Tarkovsky's poems is mysterious, comparable only to the charm of his voice. Charm is not the same as popularity. Charm is like the gravity of an extremely strong, compact celestial body, a star – it is the gravity of the text and of the poetic personality behind it. A popular poet, on the other hand, is like an asteroid or planet that obediently circles around a large readership. Tarkovsky is a poet of charm, not popularity.

*

Tarkovsky was born on 25 June 1907 in Yelisavetgrad (now Kropyvnytskyi, Ukraine) into a family with Polish roots. His father, who had a deep interest in writing and the theatre, took both his sons to readings by some of the most illustrious poets of the Russian Silver Age – a period of cultural efflorescence that began in the 1880s and ended in the first decade of Soviet rule.

In 1921, shortly after the end of the Civil War (which claimed the life of his older brother, Valery), Tarkovsky poetic career got off to a disastrous start. He and a group of friends published a poem in a Ukrainian newspaper that, by means of an acrostic, disparaged Lenin. They were apprehended and sent off to the regional capital, but Tarkovsky managed to escape from the train. For two years he supported himself as best he could, going from job to job – shoemaker's apprentice, fisherman – before moving to Moscow in 1925 and devoting himself to literature. For the next four years he attended a course run by the All-Russian Union of Poets, where he forged a number of lasting friendships, the most consequential of which was with the poet and literary theorist Georgy Shengeli (1894–1956).

Although Tarkovsky's poems did appear in print in the 1920s, the Stalinist cultural policies of the 1930s left little room for his brand of intimate lyricism, still rooted in the tradition of the Silver Age. Like many of his older, more established colleagues – including Anna Akhmatova, Osip Mandelstam and Boris Pasternak – he began to write, as the Russians say, 'for the drawer'. It was Shengeli who provided him with a literary lifeline, hiring him as a translator at the State Publishing House. There, Tarkovsky and his fellow poets-turned-translators were able to hone their craft and obliquely express their own lyrical impulses by transforming literal renditions of poems from Armenia, Georgia, Central Asia and elsewhere into Russian verse.

It was only two decades after the Second World War – where Tarkovsky was badly wounded, necessitating the amputation of a part of his leg – and a decade after Stalin's death in 1953, that a collection of his own verse, *Before the Snow* (1962), was finally permitted to appear. Its title is telling: these poems, emerging with the Thaw, seemed to have preserved the atmosphere of a warmer time through the deep freeze of the preceding quarter of a century. Irina Mashinski recalls the impact of this delayed flowering.

*

Tarkovsky gained real recognition in the 1960s, when three of his books were published. But he only became truly famous

– and, most importantly, beloved – in my time, in the 1970s and 1980s.

A witness to his late glory, I was among those who, stomping across the trampled snow in front of the Central House of Writers, desperately tried to score tickets to his 'author's evenings'. I managed to see one performance, in the early '80s. Far, far away on the stage stood a tall man with a cane, reciting poems I knew by heart – which poems they were, I don't quite remember, but I'll never forget that beautiful far-away figure of an old man with a cane, the figure of a master, whose whole aspect radiated calm dignity.

Tarkovsky's poems convey the feeling of returning to the Earth with unusual force. It's no coincidence that his second collection was titled To Earth Its Own *(1966). On the one hand, his sense of the Earth is acutely cosmic (Tarkovsky was fond of astronomy), while on the other, it's the purely physical, tactile sense of a barefoot philosopher wandering the land. 'The book and the natural world are like two halves of one nutshell, and it's impossible to separate them without touching the meat inside,' he once wrote. His language is the language of the material world. And the charm of his poems also owes to his understanding of various crafts, his love and even deification of them. Well into old age, he could easily take apart and assemble a typewriter, mend shoes, darn and embroider socks.*

For him, space and time are not the medium in which human experience takes place, they become this very experience. Even when Tarkovsky writes about the past or the future, he is writing about the present. Eternity is present in the intense experience of each moment, just as eternity was ever-present for the early Christian philosophers. The flow of time is a constant theme in Tarkovsky's poems, in which even death – of a person or of a craft – acquires the tangibility and richness of life. His verse is always in motion, never fully crystallises, never reaches (in the Aristotelian sense) its final end – it remains alive.

*

The very quality that makes Tarkovsky's verse vital in Russian, its combination of earthly texture and metaphysical movement, also enlivens *Solar Eclipse 1914: Selected Poems* (Arc Publications, 2021) – the final gift of a marvellous poet and master translator, Peter Oram. Time and again, the English versions take off from the page, following the originals with the same sense of poetic freedom – and hence the same spiritual fidelity – that guided Tarkovsky's own translations:

A moth's sudden ascent
of a ladder of light
as if someone had switched on
his fluttering flight.

Memories of Peter, who passed away in 2019, haunted us as we read this selection – perhaps nowhere more so than in his version of 'In Memory of Friends', a poem written in 1945, forty-four years before Tarkovsky's own death on 27 May 1989. It begins:

I didn't really have that many friends,
they died, they died, and I don't really know
when their last moments came, nor do I know
which paradise I could entrust them to,
to which earth to entrust their cold remains.

At the end, Tarkosvky wonders, 'Whom can I tell which way the wind is blowing, / how green the grass is or how blue the sky?' The answer is: us, his circle of readers, which our friend Peter has generously, brilliantly broadened and extended into the future:

I was born so long ago...

I was born so long ago
that there are times when I
can hear somewhere above me
freezing waters rolling by.

But I lie on the river bed
and I may sing my song
with sprouting grass, with sifted sand
but do not move my tongue.

I was born so long ago
that I can speak no more
but dream about a city
upon a stony shore,

and I lie on the river bed
and, through the waters, far
above, I see a tall house, lights,
the green glow of a star.

I was born so long ago.
But should you ever try
to cover with your hands my eyes
then that would be a lie.

I lie upon the river bed:
I can't hold onto you
for if I blindly followed you
that would be lying too.

Two Poems

ARSENY TARKOVSKY & PETER ORAM

Moth

A moth's sudden ascent
of a ladder of light
as if someone had switched on
his fluttering flight.

He opens his booklet
of wonders – he must
have powdered his wings
with heaven's blue dust.

In the transparent flask
of his abdomen.
flows the blood of another
world's denizen.

I could be in his body
but dare not displace
this miniature pharaoh's
resting-place.

Words

A word is just a shell, a skin,
an empty sound, no more,
and yet a strange flame burns within
its pink, pulsating core,

intense, alive, a throbbing vein,
yet you don't realise
the wonder of each word you write
revealed before your eyes.

Each holds the power of centuries:
if you're a poet, if you
are sure, quite sure you have no choice,
no other path will do,

don't write of things unknown, of love
or battles in advance,
avoid predictions, and don't summon
death – don't take a chance,

for though each word is just a shell,
is just a skin, it stores
your destiny – waits, hones its blades
in every line of yours.

Glitch City

PADRAIG REGAN

On the 12 June 2016, I was sitting in Woodworkers, watching – through the huge windows at the front of the pub – rain come down so hard it seemed to pixelate the façade of Benedicts Hotel on the other side of Bradbury Place. It was only after a few minutes of watching that I realised the windows were open and what I had mistaken for glass was, in fact, just air. I thought about windows: about the fact that when they are fulfilling their function most successfully is also when we are most oblivious of their presence, which means, in a sense, that one of the functions of a window is to impersonate its own absence. And I thought about glass: about how it is neither, in physical terms, a solid nor a liquid, lacking the crystalline structure of a solid, but whose molecules cannot move like those of a liquid. The term for this is 'amorphous solid', though 'glassy solid' is an acceptable, if slightly old-fashioned, alternative.

I was trying to work out if there was potential in thinking about glass as a queer material, insofar as its physicality forces us to confront the fact that the categories we receive as common knowledge – matter as solid, liquid or gas; gender as male or female; sexuality as gay or straight – are heuristic at best and cannot account for the true complex variety of being, and introduces into those systems of categorisation a disruptive new term defined only in relation to itself, bending that system around its own material needs. Which lead me to consider if I could push this line of thought a little further and suggest that glass may be an exemplar of a certain *erotic* embodiment, a kind of sluttish, self-effacing passivity, and whether this could help us to imagine new forms of political agency, not based on assertions of individual self-presence, but on more circumspect and generous principles of transparency and reflection.

I thought about this and then I didn't – a bore of noise came crashing down the stairs from the poolroom and caused the whole thought to snap (or evaporate might be a better word, seeing as it has, eventually, condensed on this page). There was a rugby match on, and the upstairs section of the pub was so full of men that an overflow of bodies had accumulated everywhere: in the smoking area out the back, in the toilets, and around the bar of the downstairs room where I was sitting. And these men were performing that particular (I don't use this word accidentally) occupation of space – the broad gestures, the open legs, the shouting – that straight men do to assert not just their own gendered and sexual selves, but also the rights which emanate from their gender and sexuality: to be recognised as the owners of space, on whose caprice the rest of us may be permitted to remain.

*

I had woken up that morning to reports of a mass shooting in Florida. As I went about my day, more details about the scale and nature of the violence filtered through. In the early hours of the morning (between two and five local time) Omar Mateen had killed 49 people and injured 53 others in Pulse Nightclub, Orlando. A few days later, there was a small vigil for the victims at City Hall. There, I met my friend Caitlin, and we hugged and there was something in the way we hugged that felt as though each of us was trying to communicate our own personal reaction to this tragedy – for me, it was an attack on the queer community (the only grouping to which I feel any allegiance); for her, it was the most recent manifestation of an ongoing pattern of gun violence that had marked the life of her country for decades – while also trying to acknowledge that the other's reaction was just as felt and valid. Belfast being a small city with a proportionally small gay community, there were many people there I recognised, including a boy I had been friendly with at school, but hadn't seen much of since. I asked him if his boyfriend was coming and he explained that his boyfriend, who was only semi-out, wouldn't have felt comfortable at such a public event. Under normal circumstances I would have judged him for this, I would have thought that surely his obligation to my one-time friend should have outweighed his sense of shame; but after the shooting, I understood that this reaction was symptomatic only of my own empathetic limitations, and that the closet was, after all, not an anachronism but still an effective tool in our defensive arsenal.

*

But this was then still the future. I moved to the back of the bar in the hope that it might be a little quieter and looked at a photograph on the exposed brick wall: it was an old school photo, wider than it was tall and filled with the grey faces of three or four hundred boys arranged in disorderly rows. I had looked at this photograph many times before I realised that it was from my own school. By my time, the empty space behind them was filled with a squat, rectangular gym which had already aged into only partial use, but the pointed sandstone window frames of the nineteenth century admin block were just as I remembered and the crest embossed on the white mount was the same Lamb of God and Keys of Heaven I had worn on my chest for seven years. These boys would have been old men by the time I had first set foot in the space where they once posed for the camera. Most likely, some of them were dead.

As I looked at the photograph, I noticed a seam running down its middle, which suggested that the panoramic aspect of the image I was looking at was created by stitching together two different exposures. And, as I followed this seam from the grey complexities of clouds above the boys' heads and into the black mass of their uniforms, I noticed that one boy's face had been bisected and he had lost half of himself in the time it took for the photographer to move his camera fifteen feet or so to the right.

And in a way, I empathised with him; or I projected onto him my own occasional desire to slip away from the world and my own embodied presence within it. A desire which, at that moment, I felt acutely; and which I can trace back to the site in which this boy achieved its fulfilment, where I spent my days surrounded by people whose difference from me was enforced (by myself as much as them, I will admit) as an essential factor in the development of identity; by which I mean that I was subjected to the grinding and ordinary cruelty that the effeminate are told we should expect, and through which boys learn the practice of their heterosexuality (more so than through sex, I suspect).

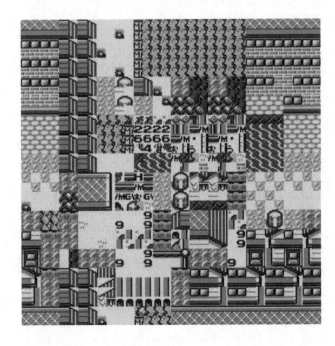

Glitch City is a generalised term used by players of the Pokémon games to refer to maps with invalid tile data. [...] Although some aspects of the source map of Glitch City are preserved (such as some tiles), most other attributes are completely changed (such as what is and is not walkable terrain).
—Bulbapedia, the community-driven Pokémon encyclopaedia

*

In the first generation of Pokémon games, it is not difficult to slip outside of the mathematics that dictates that for every entrance there must be an exit and that the two sides of every door must press against each other. By following a complex but easily replicated series of movements, it is possible to trick the game into warping you to a location that does not exist. Because the game must load something on the screen, it scrambles through its memory and comes up with a collage of tiles: grass, pavements, water, windows and bricks are blended together with numerals and scraps of indecipherable text. And all of these visual signifiers are divorced from what they represent. You can move through a Glitch City, but how and where exactly you can move cannot be discerned from the visual content on the screen: you might find yourself walking on water or, ghost-like, through a copse of trees.

It is tempting to think of the glitch as a random occurrence, to use the word to mean something like a destructive miracle. But a glitch is as much a consequence of the rules governing the system in which it happens as is the system's normal functioning; a glitch is not a moment when the system is suspended, but a moment when the system shows its freakish, unplanned depths. It shares this quality with, say, a torrential rain shower in the middle of an otherwise sunny June, or the murder of 49 queer people in a nightclub, which, despite its vital specificity, cannot be extricated from the global discursive regime in which our lives are understood to be material for theological and political debate.

*

Though I didn't go out of my way to ignore it, I didn't follow the inquest into the shooting with much attention. I had no interest in Omar Mateen, nor the attempt to reconstitute his movements and motives from the destructive traces he had left. If I wanted to, I could make an ethic of this: I could say that my responsibility as a writer is not to theorise or explicate violence, but only to attest to its unassimilable presence (and there is a chance I could convince myself to believe this). A year or so after the event, I was talking to a friend about my ideas for this essay, and he told me that the evidence pointed towards the likely interpretation that Mateen was not motivated by homophobia in any direct way, and had chosen Pulse as the theatre of his brutal display not because it was gay club but because his planned target was closed for the night. I didn't know what to do with this information: both in the sense that I couldn't work out if and how it changed the piece I was working on, and in the sense that I couldn't understand my own reac-

tion to hearing it. I think, at first, I hated my friend for telling me. I got the feeling that my friend expected it to be somehow comforting to learn that the shooting was only accidentally the biggest loss of queer lives in a single incident for more than fifty years, but (although I am sure this wasn't his intention) what I heard was my friend trying to circumscribe my reaction to the violence, to delegitimise my way of understanding the massacre through a specifically queer lens. As I've thought this through, I've come to the realisation that my initial disinterest in Mateen and his motives was, at least in part, correct. The content of his mind as he carried out the attack (as much as this can be made comprehensible) is not necessarily a significant factor in the *meaning* of the event. What gives the event its meaning are the 49 people he killed, their memory and their continuous absence, and, yes, the interpretation of the event in the consciousness of the queer community (at least in those parts of the world where we had become complacent) as a reminder that our bodily safety is, at best, still partial, unequally distributed and dependent on the permission of cisgender heterosexuals, which they reserve the right to rescind.

*

The Gameboy screen I spent a significant portion of my childhood staring at as I explored the geography of Kanto is a two-inch square made up of a film of liquid crystals laminated with polarising glass. It is capable only of straight lines and right angles which can be manipulated into jagged curves, and everything it displays is rendered in a maximum of four shades of grey.

The Gameboy's screen – like any other representational device – asks a formal question: how can you create a space through which a viewer can imaginatively move with such strict technical limitations. The solution to this problem is a drastic reduction of objects to symbols: waves are uniform stripes of grey and white, all trees are the same tree, and all buildings are the same façade stretched or contracted to give a sense of variety but never quite to the point where they could logically contain their single room interiors (which, anyway, are stored on another map so to walk through a doorway is to teleport into a parallel dimension). The glyph you pour yourself into as you play no more resembles yourself than a drawing of a landscape resembles the hand that made it.

And yet, despite this shonky, cut and pasted, bastardised attempt at depth, this environment is, for me, as deeply invested with emotional memory as the house where I grew up or the physical streets I played in as a child. There is something uncanny about seeing its textures and shapes dismembered and reconstituted as an impossible parody of itself, like when you dream of returning to a house you haven't visited for years to find its rooms are not where you left them. And something disillusioning too: you are confronted with the fact that what you took for a possible reality was only a collection of signifying units whose meaning was dependent on your imaginative participation, your willingness to believe them.

I needed a cigarette, and so I stepped out onto the street and tried to fold myself into the space beneath the concrete lip of a doorway where the water gathered like stalactites. I could have gone to the yard out the back and sheltered beneath an awning in the warm glow of a filament lamp, but, on that day, it didn't seem worth it in the calculus of risk that all queer people (but not only queer people) do as we move through the world. I thought to myself, *I'm used to this. I am as much at home in a fractured maze of visible & invisible walls as anywhere. I've learned what every little queer must learn: to be alert, to be aware of where you are & are not safe.* And there was half of me that was ashamed for thinking this, for standing in the rain.

By then Bradbury Place was doing its best impression of a river, wide and flat and not far off the point where it empties into the sea and gives up its name. To my right, I could just about see the southern end of Sandy Row, one of those gaps in my mental cartography of the city, where I rarely go and if I were to venture into I would affect a name less revealing of my background and try to minimise the outward signs of my queerness. In my mind, I swept over the west of the city, where the euphemistic 'peace walls' translate the conceptual fragmentation of Belfast into physical truth, and was reminded that the streets through which I move were, until recently, the ground of a diffuse and lengthy war (which has not resolved as such, but metastasised into a purely symbolic conflict), and, because of the intractable presence of as yet unrecovered bodies, remains an unconsecrated and unbounded cemetery.

'Ulysses' and other poems

UMBERTO SABA

translated by Patrick Worsnip

Winter Noon

In that moment just when I was happy
(God forgive me a word so vast, portentous),
who pushed my short-lived bliss almost to tears?
You'll say: 'Some pretty creature who passed by
and smiled at you.' No, a balloon, a wandering
turquoise balloon in the air's blueness,
and my native sky never so resplendent
as on that clear, cold winter noon.
A sky with just a few white wisps of cloud,
the house windows flaring in the sun,
the thin smoke of one or two chimneys,
and over all these things, God-given things,
that globe that had slipped from a boy's
careless hand (he for sure was weeping out
his pain, his terrible pain, amid the crowd)
between the Stock Exchange and the Café
where I sat and watched with glistening
eyes through the windows, now
soaring and now dipping, his pride and joy.

Ulysses

In my young days I sailed along
the coastline of Dalmatia. Island clumps,
where an occasional bird hovered
intent on prey, rose above the water,
covered with seaweed, slippery, beautiful
as emeralds in the sun. When the high tide
and night blotted them out, sails
slid off to leeward further out to sea,
to escape their treachery. Today my kingdom
is that no-man's-land. The harbour
turns on its lights for others; I am still
pushed out to sea by my untamed spirit,
my painful love of life.

Three Streets

Trieste has a street that's my reflection
when gloom and isolation fill long days:
it's called Via del Lazzaretto Vecchio.
Amid old identical buildings like hospices,
there's one note, only one, of cheerfulness:
the sea at the end of its side-alleyways.
Smelling of spices and of tar
from the desolate warehouses facing it,
it trades in netting and ropes for
shipping: one shop has as its emblem
a flag; inside there, turned towards
the passer-by, who rarely favours them
with a glance, their bloodless faces prone
over the colours of every nation,
the women workers serve their life
sentences: innocent prisoners
darkly sewing the gay banners.

In Trieste, which has sorrows a-plenty
and beauties of skyscape and landscape,
there's a rise called Via del Monte.
It starts off with a synagogue, to finish
in a cloister; half-way up the slope
a chapel stands; there the black rush
of life can be surveyed from a meadow,
and the sea with its ships and the promontory,
the crowd and the market awnings down below.

Also, beside the rise, there's a graveyard,
abandoned – they don't bury
people or host funerals now, as far
as I recall: it's the old cemetery
of the Jews, so dear to my memory
when I think of my ancestors buried, after
so much suffering and dealing, in that place,
all alike in spirit, as in face.

Via del Monte's the street of sacred affections,
but the street of love and joy
is always Via Domenico Rossetti.
This green suburban neighbourhood,
which loses a little colour day by day,
always more city and less countryside,
still keeps the fascination of its fine
years, of its first scattered villas,
of its trees in their sparse lines.
A man who's strolling it on these last summer
evenings, when the windows are
open, and each one's a belvedere,
where someone sews or reads, waiting,
might think that maybe here his darling
would bloom again with the ancient pleasure
of living, loving him and him alone;
and the pink of health return to his small son.

To William Somerset Maugham

FREDERIC RAPHAEL

Dear Mr Maugham,

Today's stylists would say 'Hi Willie!' I remain in thrall to what Shelley called 'antique courtesies'. Am I the last surviving suburban innocent for whom certain writers were distant demi-gods? Are you the last to reply in handwriting to a callow correspondent unknown to you (and who, as you remarked, omitted to date his letter)? Today, the deconstruction of literary fame is a noisy industry. Biographers are as quick to muddy renown as to displace attention onto their own verbiage. Yesterday's masters totter on pedestals that double for pillories. For all their disparagements, you continue to be more readable than your critics. Literary assayers have rarely rated you highly. I recall that in 1944 Cyril Connolly spoke up, against the current vogue, for *The Razor's Edge*. Thirty years before, an earlier pundit had been surprised by the merits of *Of Human Bondage* after a sight of the proofs you were reading on the way to the Front.

The latter title does not promise that you had conned Spinoza's work *de bout en comble*; it does intimate the range of your culture. Has any delving PhD student yet sought out what you read or learned while a student in nineteenth-century Heidelberg? Odd that you never, if I remember rightly, created a German character or parodied a German phrase, as you did *par bleu* (as 'by blue') in a short story? Did your want of Oxbridge provenance have something to do with the Establishment's reluctance to embrace you? Morgan Forster, neither as prolific nor as varied, never as amusing, was welcome both in Bloomsbury and, for many years of residence, at King's College, Cambridge. 'Dadie' Rylands, the *arbiter deliciarum* of King's, entertained you gladly, and no doubt relished your porcupine wit; but you were never embraced in any quasi-Apostolic clan, though you were, as you put it, three-quarters more queer than straight. You became too successful for your own standing among the literary élite. When Edmund Wilson 'made shift' to read your short stories, his sneer was primed by your theatrical successes. Which of his plays was ever staged on Broadway (or off)?

Doubleness served you well where it mattered most: in the work. A British subject, born in the British embassy in Paris, your first language, until you were eight years old, was French. You recall being shipped to England after your parents' deaths. You called a taxi a *fiacre*. Your mother's disappearance left a lifelong trauma; her picture always at your bedside. Was her involuntary desertion relevant to a lifelong apprehension of female *mutabilité*? It was matched, whatever your dominant appetite, by the disconcerting and delectable otherness of so many of your female characters. Neither Forster nor Conrad, Hemingway nor Faulkner created such a lively variety. Your novels, stories and plays – from *Liza of Lambert,* through *Of Human Bondage, Rain, Home and Beauty, Theatre* to *Cakes and Ale* and *The Painted Veil* – have women at the heart of things, never submissive, seldom conformist, often wantonly unpredictable, rarely foolish.

Your medical training (Evelyn Waugh is alone in being recorded as addressing you as 'doctor') armed you for case by case annotation. Biographers have made little of the significance of your time at St Thomas's, not least when dissecting cadavers. The clinical requirement to be unfeeling, the better to deliver a clear diagnosis, underlies the realism of your first novel, *Liza of Lambeth.* How typical of you to report that Edmund Gosse, that dominating Edwardian pundit, continued to greet you, after you had published any number of other books, with 'Ah my dear Maugham, I so admired your *Liza of Lambert.* How wise you were never to write anything else!'

The apparent callousness of what some critic called 'the medical mode' confronted what other English writers found distasteful or – key word – unnecessary. You contrived to be outspoken without using a single vulgar word. Ignoring ideology, you peddled no cure for the human condition, money the best placebo: you rated it a sixth sense which made it possible to enjoy the other five. The doubleness of the doctor, who guards against involvement, let alone excitement, was the key to your unblinking manner. Others elaborated; you looked, listened, took note, never prescribed.

As a small, lonely, foreign-seeming boy, translated to Whitstable, where your uncle was the vicar, you were deprived not only of parental affection but also of the *netteté* of Parisian *argot*. Your tendency to cliché in English was an echo of French writers, *dans ses oeuvres,* having recourse to standard phrases. One of the early drafts of, I think, *Of Human Bondage,* has the Gallic expression 'natal day' corrected to 'birthday'. It has become a commonplace to compare you with Guy de Maupassant. Your stories, often with a sardonic twist – 'today she weighs twenty stone' – tend to be drawn, unfiltered, from the bottomless well, if not pit, of life. Your humour rejoiced in that moustachioed face, unsmiling ossature. Playing at starchy, you were amused to portray smug first-class passengers on the ship of fools who lacked the grace of those they were pleased to mock. 'At that moment I did not entirely dislike Mr Kelada' was as far as you went to side with the outsider. It was, typically, further than it seemed.

Your longer stories owed little to anyone. *The Alien Corn* was remarkable for its treatment of Jews. Is there any other English author of the 1930s, by a rated writer, that dealt so candidly with the Chosen? Here again, your sympathies were swathed in irony. The quasi-hero is a handsome, fair-haired, straight-nosed young man who could easily pass for a Gentile. The twist is that he wants nothing other than to be a first-class pianist, an allegedly common Semitic talent. His brother, whose origins are stamped on his face, wants only to play life with a straight bat, sport the old school tie, inherit what passes for the family seat in parliament.

With your usual slyness, you tell the story from the point of view of Ferdy Rabenstein, a rich, cultivated Jew. Like Proust's Swann crossed with Benjamin Disraeli, he disdains to conform, in dress or ornament, while being as cultivated as any Fellow of All Souls. You are pleased to relish his company and, by doing so, pass comment, without a direct word, on another batch of 'betters': the *literati* who, following Mr Eliot and who all else, affected Christian contempt for Jews. What classy English writer, from Dickens and Trollope, to Greene and Priestley, failed to scorn and caricature Jews? You remarked only that 'tolerance is another name for indifference'; an epigram more shrug than smirk. What better proof of unbiassed realism than to entrust your investments to that Californian Jew, beginning with A, who amply rewarded your confidence? You did have a pompous lawyer character in *Home and Beauty,* I think it was, called A. Braham. Why not?

Your believable accounts of the misdeeds of British planters in Malaya during the *entre-deux-guerres* summoned a lasting black mark against you. Only a cad, it was said, would let the side down by revealing his compatriots to be prigs and adulterers. As for *The Letter,* based on a notorious actual case, it should never have been posted. Not only did you tell salacious tales; you were said to have abused the hospitality of guileless colonials. Who can doubt that they rejoiced in entertaining famous company? Were you greatly dismayed to be ill-regarded by face-savers in the UK or its imperial possessions? You left it to Kipling, whose work you told me you admired, to endorse imperial conceit. Whatever tributes he paid to Gunga Din, he also gift-wrapped the white man's burden. You not only cracked the code by which the British kept certain things to themselves, you also rejoiced in mocking the pretensions it mantled. You had been the first to say, before the Great War, that the British would discover the flimsiness of what they took to be the deference of lesser breeds when they ran out of money. Constantine Cavafy warned Morgan Forster against what happens to people if, as the Greeks had, they lack the gold to subsidise their vanity. Now we know.

Noel Coward, who succeeded you as the West End's darling, was pleased, in his later days, to denounce you as a spent force, unloving and unloved. His sugary version of *Our Betters* had been his 1938 play *Cavalcade.* Flag-waving ingratiated him with the public and flaunted Britannia's dominion over palm and pine. His cinematic maritime captaincy, in *In Which We Serve,* made him some kind of a war hero. Staying up with his ship, he was rewarded with a knighthood. Your only published war work was an unsentimental story set among French peasants during the Occupation. To be made a Companion of Honour, if not measly, did more to emphasise your not receiving the O.M. than to celebrate your qualities. When Jack Priestley was granted the latter sign of royal favour, Rebecca West told me that it debased the last of those posterior initials worth having. Who else, I wonder, is or has been a Companion of Honour?

Despite (or was it because of?) his pinpricking references to your obsolescence, you asked Coward to lunch, one hot midsummer day, at the Villa Mauresque. Guileless, not to say smug, enough to accept the invitation, he was allotted an unshaded place at the head of a long table, the rest of it cooled by a lowered awning. While you and the remaining guests were served with *salade niçoise,* summery delicacies and chilled wine, Sir Noel was enthroned in the full sun of a Riviera noon where he alone was favoured with roast beef, horseradish, roast potatoes, Brussel sprouts and a full-bodied claret. The true blue knight, you told him, deserved a genuine English Sunday lunch.

Coward's sexual appetites were more discreetly, and more thoroughly, indulged than yours. Thanks not least to his loudly advertised, if chaste, passion for Gertie Lawrence, he and his lovers escaped the kind of scandal which your 'secretary' Gerald Haxton excited, back in the 1920s, by making blatant advances to some young person in – can it have been? – the Natural History Museum. '*Tous les goûts sont dans la nature*' was your seemingly impersonal apology for what had done for Oscar Wilde. You had the courage, at the time of his martyrdom, to be a signatory to a petition on his behalf. It left you forever alert to how society can enjoy a wit's Yoricking for a while and then, as you put it, crumple him like a piece of wastepaper and chuck him in the bin.

Haxton's arrest was not publicly connected to you. There was a gentleman's agreement – engineered, was it, by your insufferable barrister brother Frederic, later Lord Chancellor? – not to make too much of it provided he, an American citizen, left England and never came back. You already owned the Villa Mauresque; it now became your permanent home. When married to Syrie, the mother of your only daughter, Liza, you had a smart Mayfair address: Hill street, was it? Once Haxton had been denied entry to the country, you visited London alone, quite regularly, but never again had an English residence. Might it be that Max Beaverbrook's diplomacy had some part in saving Haxton's bacon? Years later, the Beaver was blamed for having lured you into the revelations, hardly startling by today's standards, in the volume you called *Looking Back.* It was loudly serialised in *The Sunday Express. Donnant-donnant?*

Born abroad, as were Cavafy, Lawrence Durrell and Kipling, whatever pride you took in your nationality, you lacked nostalgia for home ground. Embarrassed by your poverty, even after you began to be successful and were invited to vivify the company at Edwardian country house parties, you regarded the vanities of your compatriots, grand or parochial, with persistent scorn: 'We see life in the raw at our golf club' (*For Services Rendered*). Your diction and style were indelibly in period – you are the last person I ever heard use 'omnibus' to designate a form of transport – but rectitude doubled for irony: the more proper your tone, the more scathing the nuance.

Brother Frederic was a particular target. Deny that you had him in mind when you wrote that judges should have a roll of toilet paper on the haughty desk in front of them, to remind them of what they have in common with the rest of humanity. Did someone tell you of the occasion at the Savile Club when Frederic, a man of no great stature, was being wontedly self-important? Maurice Richardson, an amateur boxer of some strength, picked him up and sat him, legs dangling, on the high mantelpiece and said, 'Sit there and tick away till someone comes and rescues you' and left the room.

When I was lucky enough to be your guest for tea at the Villa Mauresque, you quoted Kipling's 'What know they of England who only England know?' At the time, October 1954, he was out of style, but you did not doubt his qualities. Although *The Razor's Edge* dealt, with surprising and sustained respect, with oriental philosophy (the long passage bracketed to allow incurious readers to resume further on), you renounced India as a topic Kipling had made his own. You never mentioned Forster, so far as I know, in essays or in conversation. *A Passage to India* is an undoubted classic but I suspect that its adroit squeamishness, when it came to what happened, or not, in the Marabar Caves, you took to be as much artful as art. Subtlety and funk can be heads and tails of an author's wish to tease the knowing while offering no offence to the censorious. Tired of concocting heterosexual romances, Forster renounced publishing fiction. His one 'gay' novel, *Maurice*, a squeamish expression of coming out, was withheld until after his death. It is no great argument for candour. You were unstinting in your praise of *The Old Wives' Tale*: 'Arnold (Bennett) has written a masterpiece'.

Medical training, crossed with admiration for the tartness of French prose, disposed you not to flinch from any aspect of the human comedy. *Powder Puff Percy* was a brief example of your ability at once to pander to readers' appetite for deriding suspected pansies, as my father's generation called them, and to deplore their narrow-mindedness. The Leavisite charge of 'immaturity' – meiotic for queerness, especially regarding W.H. Auden – was never your style, but you conceded something by declaring El Greco's genius to be decorative, not to say flash.

Scrutiny, the Leavises' school mag, paid no heed to your novels, but it went out of its way to dismiss *Don Fernando,* a memoir of youthful travels in Spain. It was said to show how superficial your knowledge of the country and its culture. *Don Fernando* never pretended to be other than a distant cousin to *Old Calabria* by Norman Douglas. You knew the old rascal, I recall, in Capri: was he not the subject of your story about a man who decided to spend everything he had and then commit suicide at sixty-five and then, at sixty-five...? *Don Fernando* is memorable for your description of going with a young prostitute who, when undressed, proved to be no more than a child. You asked what had led her to go on the streets. She said, '*Hambre*'. Hunger. You gave her money and went back down the stairs.

George Steiner liked to quote Paul Valéry on '*la profondeur de la surface*'. Your disinclination to describe the inner lives or thoughts of your characters endorsed the view that noting word and deed trumped affectations of psychological insight: better Stendhal than Virginia Woolf. Your preference for following characters around, rather than building crenelated verbal castles, disposed you to find Henry James's fiction so stuffed with refinement as to lack any relevance to the come-and-go, rough and tumble, of human intercourse. H.J.'s snub, when he failed to include you in that pre-Great War list of young writers he deemed worthy of attention, was repaid by your disdain for his stories. You declared them so swollen with nuance that next to nothing happened; he canned beans but never spilt them.

You saved your sharpest shafts for H.J.'s darling, Hugh Walpole. You less depicted than picked him to pieces in *Cakes and Ale.* The character of Alroy Kear (how many people recognised the pun on *Kir Royal?*) nailed bestselling Walpole as a literary climber of shameless agility and small wit. That you did yourself no favours in your first personal guise was at once candid and prophylactic: portraying yourself as a crosspatch, you anticipated the knockers by knocking yourself. Walpole is said to have been mortified by your scorn for him and his work. After happening on his *The Inquisitors,* I was surprised to find how eerily entertaining it was; sorry about that.

The nicest story about Walpole as a handsome young person is that he as good as invited Henry James to, as they used to say, take advantage of him. H.J. is said to have responded, 'I can't, I can't'. The brevity was as ambiguous as it was untypical. Was the denial moral or physical? That 'obscure hurt', incurred when James slid down a fence in his Bostonian youth, was never specifically diagnosed. Did it render him literally impotent or did the obscurity lie in the neutralising effect on his appetites? Max Beerbohm sentenced him to be remembered, with a smile, as the stout stooper in the *Hotel des Trois Couronnes* sniffing the shoes left outside doors for cleaning, in order to deduce what was happening inside. You told me that you had recently visited Max in Rapallo. 'I was sh-shocked at the change in him. He seemed a very old man. Of course he *is* a very old man. He must be at least eighty. But he l-looked a hundred and fifty.'

Unlike Forster, Henry James was never silenced by inability at least to imagine heterosexual passion. *Portrait of a Lady* was a transvestite fantasy of the beautiful Isabel surrounded by vivid varieties of male beastliness or inadequacy. H.J. subscribed so thoroughly to the conceits of the British that they could not but think well of him. Unlike the raffish Frank Harris, he dined many times more than once at the best tables in London and took care to be so replete with refinements that manners passed for manliness. There was sweet irony that you can but have relished in the fact that H.J.'s humiliation

on the 1895 first night of *Guy Domville* coincided with that of Oscar Wilde's triumphant *The Importance of Being Earnest.* Having read most of James's work, I remain slightly surprised that Leavis should made him the culminating master of the Great Tradition of English fiction. I ain't much of a Janeite either.

Your successes in the Edwardian West End were capped by that *Punch* cartoon showing the shade of Shakespeare sulking at the sight of playbills advertising your work in four theatres in the same season. Many writers have been pleased to assume that theatrical and cinematic success amounted to something little better than prostitution. It may pay well but, they like to hold, it requires no more than a willingness to be what H.J. called (after his thudding failure) 'base'. That rare Jamesian monosyllable said it all, but not quite enough: in neither theatre nor the movies is success as easy as it is convenient for the condescending to presume.

You were Tiresian enough to bat for both sides. That passion for a beautiful American actress, with whom you broke only when she became pregnant by another man, may have been decisive in disposing you to play safe, though never as safe as you hoped, by relying on your own sex for pleasure, if never for love. When Haxton died, you were, it is said, deeply bereaved. In public, you said only that he had been 'useful', not least because he had a facility for luring strangers into revealing conversation, which you were not slow to record. It became a regular lament of yours that you had never known reciprocal love (scarcely Syrie's fault, was it?). Your house guest Cyril Connolly was bold, and charming, enough to dare to greet your lamentations with '...although the night grew chilly, no one cared to poke poor Willie'.

The young Paddy Leigh Fermor earned no laurels when, seeking to entertain the company, he imitated a stammering man. You were touchy enough, on that occasion, to say 'goodbye' rather than 'good night'. He would, you explained, be on his way to the station before you came down to breakfast. Stories of your sarcasm are the small change of small people. Beverley Nichols, in blazer, neck-square and white flannel bags, affected to be hurt when you greeted him, as you were on your way to your desk (I was at the auction where Godfrey Winn bid £500 for it), with 'Good morning, B-Beverley. You're looking very s-s-spruce!'

The story I like best is of when you went with Alan Searle, in the long evening of your days, to the Hôtel de Paris, in Monte Carlo, for dinner. On the way in, Alan Searle spotted George Axelrod sitting in the foyer. With his usual (as I experienced it) grace, Searle whispered to you that it would be appreciated if you were to say a word or two to the author of *The Seven Year Itch,* a current Broadway smash hit. You went over to George and said, 'I am t-told that you are a very brilliant young p-playwright and you have just had a g-g-great s-s-success. All I can say is, thank G-god I'm too old to g-give a shit'.

I like to imagine that George agreed to be amused. We went with him and Joan one evening to have dinner with Christopher Isherwood and Don Bachardy in Santa Monica. Isherwood opened the door and apologised for not having put us off; he was afraid he had rather a bad cold.

George said, instantly, 'My dear Christopher, any cold of yours is a cold of mine'. *Chapeau?*

You have never been accused of being a writer of the first rank, still less did you ever claim to be. A diligent worker, you were sometimes surprised by the speed with which the best novelists (Stendhal not least) could dash off their work, even in longhand. You yourself ceased to write books because you suffered so painfully from arthritis that you could no longer hold a pen for sustained periods. Unlike Henry James, you never had recourse to dictation. The stammer, I guess, would come between you and the fluency which gave your imagination its scope. Why did your facility, when it came to dialogue, never incline you to use a typewriter?

A stammer seems an odd affliction for someone who so swiftly put words into other people's mouths. Dialogue your forte, you were garrulity itself in printed and performed work. You shared your misfortune with my contemporaries Ken Tynan and Jonathan Miller. Both spoke with little hesitation when publicity and acclamation were available. You had the wit to turn what seemed a disability into some kind of asset when, at the dinner at the Garrick to celebrate your eightieth birthday, you got to your feet to respond to the toast to your health. You began by saying 'C-c-contrary to what others might fear, reaching my present age had its c-c-compensations.' The Old Party, as you came to call yourself, opened his mouth to go on, it seemed, but no words came out. The silence became all but embarrassing. You stood there and stood there and then you said, 'I'm just trying to think what they c-could p-possibly be'. Relief and admiration charged the ovation that followed. Timing is of the essence in stand-up.

I have a notion – a phrase you used more than once – that your stammer was the result of a kind of mental chicane: the multiplicity of voices and languages in your brain raced, collided and jammed when it came to speech. I advanced this theory, rather generously I thought, when taken to lunch, by one of today's Alroy Kears, with one of your imminent biographers, a titled youngish lady. In the style of today's allegedly classless Britain, she appropriated my contributions but her bibliography did not mention my several times reprinted

monograph about you and your work, a pretty compliment, as you might have said.

One evening in the late 1950s, I was able to return your hospitality. Hearing that you were in London, I arranged game of bridge at Crockford's. Kenneth Konstam and Edward Mayer and Guy Ramsey made up the four. You wore careful glasses and played with modest competence. My little tribute did something to discharge a long debt. *Of Human Bondage* changed my life. In the days before television, a fifteen-year-old suburban only child had little to do but read. I went through my parents' library (except for that complete Dickens) with greedy curiosity. When my mother had mumps, I was banned from going in to see her. I had literally all day to read that illustrated edition my parents had brought from New York.

It included an image of the lusty Miss Wilkinson undressing down to her stays. She was supposed to look a fright, but I saw her as quite stimulating. Your Philip Carey spoke directly to me as no other fictional character ever had (though C.S. Forester's Captain Hornblower furnished wartime fantasies of life on the ocean wave). My miseries at school could, you taught me, be turned to literary use, provided – the proviso was of the essence – what was made of them was self-deprecating. One had to make a model of oneself and then be sure to be merciless in the moles-and-all department. I had always wanted to be a writer; you taught me how: work, work, work; and never wait for inspiration.

Is it graceless to remark that, when I went back to *Of Human Bondage,* after my mother gave me a handsomely bound copy, I was dismayed at some of the awkward locutions it contained? I had something of the same surprise when re-reading *Le Rouge et le Noir.* In both masterpieces, the vividness of the characters made grammarian's quibbles irrelevant to the pleasure they continue to give. Flaubert said of Balzac, '*Quel écrivain, s'il savait écrire,*' [What a writer had he known how to write]. So much for Flaubert, you might have said, while never denying him to his place in the sun.

Merci, maître.
Frederic Raphael

'A Spider's Web' and other poems

SUJATA BHATT

Paul Klee's House, Dessau

The spiders have chosen
the most beautiful room
and now they're here to stay.
You may not see them
but they have already found
their favourite corner,
high up on the ceiling where it's always dark,
high up where they can always hide.
The walls around them painted in shades
of violet blue, violet pink and grey.
I see shades of blue grey, blue lavender,
a hint of aubergine,
dusty brownish pale pink
and subdued violet.

I think of a garden in summer dusk –
birdsong after rain –
shadows deepen across hortensia, larkspur –
hushed voices rise and fall
with a gentle intensity – shadows darken
as the moon contradicts the wind.

Sometimes Words Dissolve into Sounds

Sometimes words dissolve into sounds
and sounds begin to inhabit colours,
while colours want to grow
into fish or birds.

Often when Paul Klee
worked in his beloved atelier
in Dessau amidst pine trees
he would play the violin for hours
before beginning a new painting.

Mozart was one of his favourites.

He kept the door locked.
The cat was his only listener.

South of the Elbe

East of the Elbe lives the hooded crow.
West of the Elbe, the carrion crow.

I have travelled from East to West
and back again from West to East.
I have travelled endlessly.

All morning I watched these hooded crows:
how slender they are, how elegant
beneath the tall pine trees.
The pine trees are also slender
and the wind makes them sway easily.
Sometimes it seems as if that's all they want to do:
just sway from side to side
while the crows flick through pine needles and grass.

I can watch the light for days,
how it moves between the crows and the trees.

My mind wanders:
The hooded crows take me back
to Maninagar –
the pine trees to Maine.

Now this poem could go almost anywhere.

A Spider's Web

Paul Klee, Spinnennetz, 1927

A spider's web has taken over the night.

Imagine:
a spider's web across the vastness of night.

Silence has come to rest here
as if it were one of the angels.

Can we banish the unspeakable?
Can we keep the 'unheard of' unheard?

What I mean by silence
is the absence of human sound,
the absence of any sound
made by humans.

And yet, a certain non-silence
grows out of this silence.

Don't we always listen for something?

What do we listen for
when we seek out silence?

In the distance, pine trees are tiny
or have they shrunk?
It's a distance
that comes closer and closer to us.

Imagine: you can hear
a soul calling out to the universe.
Perhaps the soul of a bird
or the soul of a tree.

And now: sunrise, moonset –
young saplings – darkest brown earth.
Dawn shadows, pine green shadows –

Patches of pine green cover the ground,
stain the freedom of pine cones.
Fertility within decay.
So much is hidden, so much waits to be seen.
The dreams of pine needles
stolen by birds.
Everything is itself and more.

And the sky, not to be outdone,
summons the wind, scatters clouds,
spills morning blue everywhere.

The spider is here
somewhere in the grass. The spider hides
between blades of grass
while its freshly made web remains
untouched – taut yet supple
against the slightest breeze.

Amber light falls across the tiny trees,
the saplings – amber light rich with September
seeps through the spider's silk.

Moments of equilibrium,
moments of suspense
as the equinox hovers on the horizon.

It was simply the movement
of what I call silence,
a gesture that reminded me of an angel.

Does that already conjure
an angel for you?

Everything is connected to everything.
Everything grows into something else.

Fine lines depicting the sun's rays
just like the lines depicting pine needles
just like the lines creating the spider's web
just like the lines that could reveal the spider –

the spider we do not see,
the spider we can only imagine.

The Beauty of *Rien*

But 'rien' is such a lovely word! Better than nothing.
  — Adam Zagajewski

The beauty of the word *rien* –
The richness of the letter 'r'
when Édith Piaf sings

Non, rien de rien
Non, je ne regrette rien...

The full moon turns gold.
This road cuts through terra rossa.
And here we see
the beauty of the letter 'R'
as it stands tall and green
by the white villa
in Paul Klee's painting.

Tall and green and solidly firm
you might say it's almost stern
this capital letter 'R'
as it stands guard over someone's dreams.

Dreams may be full of *rien*
but they live on nonetheless
persistent as they sing along
with Édith Piaf.

Then...

BRIAN MORTON

In the field below the house, the land girls worked with their backs to the sea, as they'd been told. When they heard the drone of engines they bent over, hitched up the skirts of old coats and watched back between their legs. The boys, further down the field, looked at the girls' backsides and threw rogue potatoes at the prettiest ones. The plane came in low past Strone point, so low it looked like it was readying to land. It jerked sharply up when freed of its load and then soared high and wide to avoid the first bounce as the barrel-shaped thing skited twice, three times, four, five across the water, before thumping into the old ship's side. The girls would wait till the hollow boom arrived to match the final splash and quiver. After the first time, the man who'd ordered them to work facing the hill came back and told them they'd seen nothing. Tom Lamont said he'd seen Janet McGrath's knickers, but wouldn't tell a soul.

These things happened long ago, but they are still, as they say, the speak of the place...

The farmhouse sits on a shelf of flat ground, protected from the wind by the hill's shoulder. It long ago absorbed most of the outbuildings, but a byre and shed are still attached. There is a tiny upstairs, two small rooms with archer-slim windows looking out over the loch. In front and to the right, a giant beech, completely hollow, where the barn owls nest. Walk past it when there are chicks and the tree hisses like a leaky gas cylinder as the young birds vent irritation and alarm. Step out on a winter night and the adult birds ghost silently across the lazybeds and screech at the intrusion. The open byre is a second home, with clutches of eggs alternated between the two. Approach the door unwarily and a white shape manifests in the dark rectangle, a Fuseli nightmare. Feathers brush the face. The eyes pass through, felt as a tingling hollowness.

We came, and vowed we would never leave. The house was modest, but for us it was the magical *domaine* in *Le Grand Meaulnes*, the lost but always recoverable place of dreams. I felt roots go down the moment I arrived and tear the day we had to go. I thought of it like Restif de la Bretonne's *bonne vaux*, Samuel Palmer's paradisal valley in Kent, or Thorncombe in John Fowles's *Daniel Martin*. In the novel, Martin describes it as a place 'outside the normal world, intensely private and enclosed, intensely green and fertile, numinous, haunted and haunting, dominated by a sense of magic that is also a sense of a mysterious yet profound parity in all existence'. True and relevant in every way but one. The land was scarcely fertile, rough scrub and juncus clinging on to a sour podzol that showed pale, leached horizons as the spade went down and down. No worms, no smell of vitality.

We grew nothing until the third spring when accident revealed that the mounded area northwest of the house was the old midden. The nettles should have given it away. Once they were ripped out, the soil below was a rich as Dundee cake. It took two years of sweetening with lime, kelp and leafmould to bring it into heart, after which it produced potatoes of prodigious size, onions that made you cry just to look at them, and cabbages the size of heads.

Running alongside the kitchen garden was a little carved-out *alt* or combe, with an angle of drystone wall in it, going nowhere in one direction and nowhere in another. In the angle, I put a seat and a rhombus of dry standing, pebbles from the beach. I half-buried in them a convex safety mirror, the kind they use on London Underground to watch for would-be suicides or later arrivers wrestling with closing doors. It was meant to serve as a reflecting pool, but it became our planetarium. On a clear night Venus would burn in it like new hope. Shooting stars elongated across the meniscus, the moon too dazzling to look at.

There used to be many houses. The ruins of Dalbuie itself were within the farm, reduced to shoulder height, with just one intact but glassless window. Walk the fields and the footprint of many more became obvious. Oblong scatters of shaped stone sit on platforms too regular and contrary to the lie of the land to be natural. At the start of the twentieth century, there were 800 dwellers within the parish. Then there were less than a dozen: two families, a couple who tend the clan headquarters, and an elderly psychic medium who stopped his car to look appraisingly at our outlines and tell us that our aura was strong today and that we'd be meeting an old friend before the week was out. He regularly saw my grandmother standing behind me. She was tall and black-haired, which would have been a delight to her, for in life she was short and auburn.

Was the house haunted? We never saw anything, but from the week we moved in I began to dream of the same family: a woman with faded red hair, pregnant, always standing at the front door with a cigarette held, unsmoked, in her right hand, the elbow cupped in her other. She seemed to stare out into the darkness. Up in the fanks a powerfully built man whose hair was permanently wet, the scalp showing in multiple partings or *sheds* that are said to be a sign of the drowned; another man, or the same, who stood, again always at night, in the crook of wall down in the combe, a dog at his feet, and his face lifted to the sky. And there was a girl, the only one dreamed in daylight, also red haired, with a wide backside and wet lips, who seemed to be laughing or teasing. I opened the back door one day to find a car parked at the gate and two women taking photographs.

It was the red-haired girl, or her descendant, come for the first time to see where her grandfather had lived. Her sister was with her. Both were in the middle of divorces. The one seemed free and bantering, flirtatious, the older resentful and suspicious, invitation in the one and an unspoken accusation in the other, as if we had stolen a birthright. The red-haired girl came back once or twice.

Without knowing why, I identified with the wet-haired man. Drowning seemed part of the charism of the place. When the rain fell on the tin roof, it was as if the whole world were washed away in some final inundation, a submarine noise that deadened everything. Divers know the loch for the number of wrecks it holds, some of them scuttled ships that limped back from convoys to die close to home. The wrecks are infamous for conger eels, mad-faced things as girthy as a thigh, with Alien teeth. The loch claimed and held bodies and gave them back only slowly and unwillingly. We searched for two days for a woman tourist who had gone walking on the other side, having taken a packed lunch from her b'n'b. We searched along the hill, right to the knife-edge *arête* that would have driven any sane walker back and down, but there was no sign of her. A helicopter whirred up and down like a crane fly for a time and then left.

It was two years, during which time the family had applied to have her declared dead, before she rose up out of the loch and laid herself on the rocks by Ardkiel, her bag still with her. The place is known for what are supposed to be Viking graves, men who succumbed to wounds at the Battle of Largs, but almost certainly older. Maybe she died by the side of a burn and had to wait till a winter spate saddled up a kelpie who took her on one last mad ride down.

The following spring we watched from the opposite shore as a saloon car bounced slowly along the track. Three figures got out, not in country clothes, and walked slowly – town shoes, too – to the 'Viking' graves, where they stood in a huddle for ten minutes before walking slowly back to the car. There's often activity on 'the other side'. Kilgortan is one of the remotest crofts in mainland Scotland. From us, it was ten minutes in a boat across from, even against the tide and shearing winds, but a conservative three hours by road. Argyll's coastline – we bore everyone with this nugget – is longer than the coastline of France, a fractal landscape.

These were safe waters during the war. Injured and secret ships were hidden here, out of reach of bombers, largely out of sight. It was a good place to test new weapons. Older men who were children at the tiny one-room school on the loch road remember the morning when a torpedo flopped up onto the beach just below the classroom window and lay there like a dying salmon, its propeller still fizzing the water. When the sailors came to haul it away, Miss Tocher screamed at them from the road. She used words some of them had never heard before. The men in the boat wrestled shame-faced with the thing, under withering verbal fire. When they at last left, Miss Tocher came back inside and continued reading *Wee Macgreegor* to the boys – it was a school without girls for several years – without missing a beat.

The schoolhouse lay empty for years, until it was bought by a retired mathematics professor who spent his days tapping out nuclear disarmament pamphlets – Xeroxed copies lay in yellowing piles in the local library and doctor's surgeries – that referred more often to Nostradamus than to Einstein or Edward Teller. He also reported UFO sightings. We saw them, too, dark, lenticular clouds that formed in minutes above the hills opposite, looking black and solid, shaped and then dissipated by the same wind.

After he died, the roof fell in and foxes screamed and yipped in the strewn schoolroom, their smell detectable even from the road. It was a place we went often. The bow of sheltered water that cradles the school held huge flocks of eider in winter, murmuring softly through the short afternoons and evenings like blacktied clubmen. In the summer, in the shallows below the house, where the dummy torpedo is said to have fizzed ashore, the water blooms with brittle stars, far more delicate and numerous than fleshy starfish. On peaceful nights, I dream the stars drifting over a dead face, sentient black filaments.

Behind the house, hard to see unless you were on it and easier to see from the other side of the glen is a thin track that runs against the grain of contour lines, rising from the beach to a dropped shoulder at the head of the glen. This was the coffin road, along which dead chiefs were carried by young men of the clan for burial at Kilmun. On summer nights, an occasional group of walkers would pass by, murmuring quietly. Bent forward against the incline, it was easy to see them as mourning, their backpacks blending together to suggest a bier.

Seen from the other side, the path is arrow-straight, punctuated further up by three soft indentations on the hill side. Local archaeologists – who're still slowly mapping the place – argue over whether these are charcoal-burners' platforms from maybe two centuries back, in the time before sheep, when the area would have been more extensively wooded, or whether they are Neolithic pedestals. Possibly, both, for like all landscapes, this one is a palimpsest, and thing are often older than they appear, rather than younger.

The sheep changed everything, here as elsewhere. Mostly they stay high, where grass remains plentiful in damp, mild winters, but the sick ones used come down and gravitated to the house to die. We found them in the yard, off their legs, reeking of urine, but still heavingly alive. The gamekeeper, who only loved his pheasants – loved them unto death, as it were – came round grudgingly, popped a .22 into the head, and dragged the carcase away. He never took them far. We'd waken to see a row of hoodie crows sitting on a dyke, debating who had first dibs. Jim and his pheasants. We used to say of him that if you wanted a favour done, you needed long tail-feathers and a white ring round your neck, like a hybrid of vicar and showgirl.

The sheep provided occasional diversions. On Easter morning, 2008, the children came in excitedly to say that there were lambs, lambs, and that the mother had blown up. I dragged on an old brown bathrobe used when washing the dogs, slipped on a pair of sandals and followed them – *lambs, dad, lambs!* – a quarter mile up the coffin road. Down in an *alt* – too deep for the hoodies to venture; for birds of their reputation, they're markedly risk-averse – a yowe lay on her side, bloodied at the rear, two newborns nudging hopelessly at her. She had, indeed, blown up, but had given birth before expiring. The gamekeepers put out drums of grain for the pheasants, old mango tubs from the Indian restaurant market with a spring device jury-rigged underneath which the birds learned to peck to release the grain. The sheep were even better at it, but gorged until the swelling grain literally burst them open.

I slithered down into the *alt* and gathered up the unresistant lambs – I was, after all, the first living thing they'd seen – and carried them, one under each arm, back towards the house. Coming towards us was a pair of female walkers, speaking what sounded like Dutch. They stopped, looking confused and almost frightened. What had they seen? Hirsute, bearded man in brown robe and sandals, carrying lambs. Children skipping joyously behind. Easter morning. Not quite canonical, but it must have crossed their minds. We braced for gaggles of pilgrims, but none came. A bad-tempered German woman banged on the door one day, demanding a plaster, as if our ill-kempt paths were the cause of her pain. The red-haired girl drifted back, too, a pilgrim of another sort.

We left our mark in small ways. Gardening was a struggle. The gamekeeper trapped mink and stoats, so the rabbit population mushroomed. He'd lamp a few on winter nights, just to be seen to be doing it, but they were ever-present. Soft crops had to be grown in tall raised beds, but they thrived in the rich soil and we ate well, sometimes with a rabbit stew to accompany the vegetables. We found mimulus thriving in the ditch outside the schoolhouse and pulled out a few roots. It grew rampant, covering all the wet spots with monkey-faced orange flowers, clearly not catnip to the rabbits. In the little combe with the reflecting pool, where I saw the wet-haired man, I put a slick of concrete on the walls at either end and picked up the Great Bear and Orion in white quartz. I assume they're still there. On cold winter nights,

I'd stand like Peter Grimes in the angle they made, with the sky burning in miniature in the pool at my feet.

We arrived back one day to find a young man with a camera tripod, photographing the house from flattering angles. He was previous. The landlord had told no one that the estate was being broken up and sold. Divorce and bad business deals – unlike the hoodies, he had a positive addiction to risk – had driven the business to the brink of bankruptcy and his Highland plaything was being taken away. We felt the dragging imminence of exile and began looking for somewhere else to live, stoically trying to list all the ways the place had *always* felt unlucky, much as we loved it.

It did have a whiff of death about it, and a sense of holding great secrets. The estate house held a pair of what were supposedly Winston Churchill's slippers, and some of the old men claimed to have seen Churchill and Eisenhower pacing the sycamore avenue, planning D-Day. Barnes Wallis's secret weapon had been tested on the loch, with a decommissioned French battleship standing in for the Ruhr dams. The footage that survives, long declassified, must have been taken from the lower field. Slowed up, with the plane's propellers turning as lazily as ceiling fans, it has a nightmare quality. We found that if you stood on the recumbent standing stone at the field's edge you had exactly the same view as that wartime cameraman. Recumbent stones seem to follow us. There is another at the new place, also said to have brought bad luck.

The week we left, they started to winch the first of the bouncing bombs up out of the loch, crusted concrete ovals, Olmec heads recovered from a drowned city. On the last night, with the family already gone ahead and just the van to wait for, the rain fell as never before. I stood outside, washed of the dust and dirt, watching the track dissolve in muddy runnels. (The van next day only made it up and back down by a whisper, bouncing dangerously in the ruts.) As I stood, looking across at the hill, a scoop of sodden earth slipped downward, leaving a deep red scar like a torn knee. I sneaked back only once to see the old place, and it still hadn't healed. Nothing has.

W

After Tony Harrison

CAITLIN STOBIE

Last May I cycled to the cemetery
to see old graffiti, the Vs, your task.
All I found was dog shit and dried lilies,
then drifting litter: a surgical mask.

Who am I to write this reply?
Thin slices of an accent, southerner
by way of Africa: best believe I,
too, hate grave advice from foreigners.

But someone has to start with the questions.
Again I try, fail, trying to go on.
Each year brings more floods and man-made seasons;
what if we united, but did it wrong?

Walking long ago, counting cracks, I asked
Why's the street wet? to a boy from a band.
He pointed his free hand. A drunk's turned back.
If you were a man, love, you'd understand.

On Saturdays all men came out alleys
to grope the slippery centre of Leeds.
The city's never been so lively
we chanted, dodging vomit every week.

Tony, you know what's meant when I say 'all'
and 'men'. For in the Brude and Chunk you'd see
– even in Wharf's safest toilet stall –
them slits slashed clean between two widened Vs.

In '85 it was swear words lads sprayed
round town. Now 'cunt' is on discount, reduced.
'The versuses of life', 'man and wife': splayed
like legs in the cubicle W.

They say in Shakespeare's day, 'cunt' was 'nothing'.
Lately, the male organ's tune is the same.
Why else, when we protest, would some men sing
Not all? Their chorus is not to complain.

Worse still are the racists, the EDL
with their own slogans of 'nothing' and 'not'.
All lives matter, they say, but they fear hell
is other people talking, taking their lot.

In the year of the rat, trafficked pangolins and bats,
lines between species were ever troubling
and as humans destroyed their habitats
the Vs and our visions were doubling.

It should not have taken a pandemic
to see that we need to set this right.
Yet between the blurring Vs came an epic
chorus chiming *Not all!* and *Mine! Mine! Mine!*

When you can't walk at night without keys between your
    fists,
what do you rhyme that with?
Where can you wander without watchmen if you're
    Black?
(The chorus warbles: *Not all! Mine! Mine! Mine!*)

We bicker and consumerist excess continues, the Vs are
Ws, too many to write –
when that man said *You wouldn't understand*,
why did I not drop his hand?

Last May, I traced letters on graves. Cee, u, en, tee.
Much ado about the bard, in your poem, Tony,
but Shakespeare leads to one more query:
if 'nothing' is sacred, then what does that make me?

Laughter bloomed. *You – you stupid animals*,
cats-ears nodded as if to say,
*you're nowt special. Blood, meat, bones, minerals:
all beasts turn to feed when they decay.*

Then it hit me: the double-u in nowt.
Same as millennials' scrawl in toilets,
but the slashed command signified now
both\holy\everything\and\jack-shit.

Like headstones leaning together, four lines
in a consonant, a cuss, or a poem
may remind us of the beasts inside –
or so I liked to hum as I headed home.

So home I ride – for some of us never
felt safe outside, for I am no bride, no double you
see (in my head the man says, *'n
anyway, love, how's about you make tea*).

No. Home to a room and view of my own,
to the place where I grandmother myself.
I doze in a rented room, alone,
old words of new worlds lining my bookshelf.

Reader, how will Leeds look next year?
When do death-tolls become a wake-up call?
When we rebuild, will we remember nowt?
Will nothing have changed at all?

André Naffis-Sahely in conversation

RORY WATERMAN

Waterman: You live in the USA, and you're married to an American, yet in one recent poem you write: 'how strange it is that it's here, / where after a decade of rootlessness, // I abandon all cravings for permanence...', which does not imply a settled spirit. What is your relationship to your current homeland? Has it at least been fertile ground for your poetry, do you think?

Naffis-Sahely: I'm a citizen of the world, not that citizenship is a political construct that satisfies our needs and aspirations. I cannot think of a single nation-state that hasn't persistently betrayed even its most loyal citizens, even when it pretends to include them: 'America never was America to me', Langston Hughes once wrote. The two cities that dominated my perspective and growth as a child and adolescent were Venice and Abu Dhabi, neither of which truly accepted me as one of their own. After dispatching its sons and daughters to the far corners of the world in search of profit for the entirety of its history, the Most Serene city of Venice is now childless, having priced nearly everyone out of the islands and into the mainland. Abu Dhabi's princes, on the other hand, consider 9 out of 10 of the people within their borders as disposable servants and I've written about that extensively. Despite a very happy twelve-year spell in the UK, recent political changes have made it abundantly clear that foreigners of my ilk are no longer tolerated. I moved to the US to be with my partner, who could not afford to move to Europe at the time we decided to be together. Following a spur of the moment decision, we found ourselves in California, whose hidden histories of racial and labour repression have attracted my interest and I have found my time in the American West intellectually fulfilling. However, my current 'homeland' has spent years running my name through terrorist databases and going through my mail. Let's not even mention the lengthy interviews by Immigration and the extended detentions. All that being said, I'm one of the lucky ones.

W: What 'recent political changes' in the UK? What do you mean by 'my ilk'? Do you really think you'd now be treated differently than you were if you still lived in the UK?

N-S: I'm talking about Brexit and the decision made by the thinnest of margins to leave the European Union. EU membership is clearly not universally positive and the institution is crying out for reforms – the lack of censure against the horrific policies put in place by Poland and Hungary's governments being a good case in point – but watching the insular dregs of the old Empire muling about 'imported labour' has been nothing short of revolting, especially since half of London has been sold off to rich foreigners. Right now I'm applying to the EU Settlement Scheme and the process is needlessly complicated. I imagine my Middle Eastern background (my ilk) will complicate the process, as it has everywhere else. An American friend of my wife's married an Irishman and he got his green card in two years. My process took five and half even though I too travel on an EU passport (Italian). There's a reason I get screened by Homeland Security in *London*.

W: To what extent did this feeling that you are unrooted – albeit 'one of the lucky ones' – inspire you to edit *The Heart of a Stranger: An Anthology of Exile Literature* (Pushkin Press, 2020)?

N-S: Exiles of one kind or another have shaped the arc of my family tree as far back as I can tell. While one of my great-great-grandfathers fled Baku in the wake of Stalin's communist takeover in 1917, relocating to the Iranian shores of the Caspian Sea, my father would later be exiled from Iran precisely for being a communist. Tales of exile tend to have a way of revealing history's subtle ironies and my intentions with *The Heart of a Stranger* were to showcase the dizzying wealth of literature produced by exiles, from ancient Egypt to the present, and open a window into the phenomenon of displacement across different cultures, religions, historical periods and political affiliations. Although the Ovidian conception of exile has taught us to see the 'Exile' as a withered husk forever longing for the branch it was unhappily torn from, I wanted to showcase an alternative genealogy of misfits, rebels, heretics, contrarians, activists and revolutionaries. Exile, this anthology argues, can be defiant, bold and uncompromising, examples set by the French communard Louise Michel on her way to the penal colony in New Caledonia; or Emma Goldman's defiance aboard the USS Buford as she was deported from the United States a century ago during the First Red Scare. In the more contemporary sections of the book, I opted to foreground texts that explicitly rejected the classificational fetishism that has jeopardised our ability to discuss so-called refugees, migrants, and asylum seekers as actual people, rather than case studies. Assuming that people can be neutrally assigned dehumanising categories is a dangerous gamble. The citizens of today can very quickly become the refugees of tomorrow.

W: Your poetic life centres on Britain: your debut collection, *The Promised Land: Poems from Itinerant Life*, was published here by Penguin in 2017, you've just served as *Ambit*'s poetry editor for three years, and you have now become the editor of *Poetry London*. I know you initially came to Britain to study, but do you feel a particularly strong connection to contemporary British poetry, if not to policy? Or is this just how things have panned out?

N-S: The United Arab Emirates, or as its former colonial masters called it, the Trucial Coast, was a British 'protectorate' for over a century and a half until it achieved independence in 1971. Since the Empire deemed it an economic backwater, albeit a strategically useful one, since it lay smack in the middle of trading routes between the upper Gulf and India, the British mostly left the local rulers free to manage their own affairs, meaning they maintained a benign image which persists to this day, thus the British occupied a culturally-influential role that far outstripped their physical presence. Given that the majority of the UAE's migrant population is drawn from the Indian Subcontinent, and that I attended Indian schools staffed by Indian teachers, the colonial imprint on my upbringing was fairly indelible. I dropped out at fifteen, partly to spare my father the onerous burden of school fees, since all migrant children were locked out of the UAE's free public education system, at which point I sat for my O and A levels at the British Council. It was therefore natural that like many from the so-called periphery I was drawn to the old centre. I suppose that makes me a good post-colonial subject. When I interviewed Deepak Unnikrishnan – whose *Temporary People* (Restless Books) will come to be seen as a seminal text for our dislocated generation – we spoke about the influences of this upbringing and he said: 'The British are good that way, they leave behind certain vestiges that you have to take and pocket.' He's right. I think my greatest single stroke of luck was that I was erroneously admitted as a 'home student' at the University of Leicester, which made continuing my education financially viable. Coincidentally, *Poetry London* was the first poetry magazine I chanced across, when a copy or two inexplicably hit the shelves of one of Abu Dhabi's lone bookshops. By then I had fallen deeply in love with the work of Louis MacNeice, W.H. Auden, Derek Mahon, Tom Paulin and Michael Hofmann – an enduring influence – but that was more of a happy coincidence.

W: A decade or so ago, you gave me a copy of Auden's *The Age of Anxiety*, and said 'I know you will have read this' – the act of a very excited young man. Hofmann's influence can be felt in the forms and tones of your collection, and while you were working on that you co-edited a volume of essays and poems on his work, *The Palm Beach Effect* (CB Editions, 2013). How important were these two, and the other poets you mention, to your formation as a poet, and do they retain that importance now?

N-S: I'd like to recapture that wide-eyed excitement, it's long gone. *The Age of Anxiety* has morphed into The Age of Terror and the implications of that have left me feeling quite sober. Still, it's a privilege to be alive in such times, when so much is at stake, it's invigorating. I never really got over Hofmann's *Acrimony* and *Corona, Corona* – and why should anyone? His memoiristic, peripatetic poems provided a map that inevitably left a deep imprint on *The Promised Land*. He was an influence I was proud to wear on my sleeve, the way Derek Walcott said young poets should, but it's also only fair that one should evolve – not outgrow, but evolve. Hofmann himself has

with his latest collection, *One Lark, One Horse*. Living in Los Angeles, a city often accused of lacking a soul, actually led me to reconnect with the work of an early love of mine, the brooding environmental prophet Robinson Jeffers, who went from being on the cover of *Time* magazine in 1932 and being hailed as Walt Whitman's true heir, to having his publisher Random House print a disclaimer in *The Double Axe and Other Poems* (1948) expressing 'disagreement over some of the political views pronounced by the poet in this volume'. Why? Because he pointed out that America's imperial ambitions would usher in a century of expansionist murder, hardly a controversial statement to make. Édouard Glissant's sharp poetic essays have been leaving their mark of late and I hope to translate a volume of them soon.

W: Jeffers had, for example, opposed US involvement in the War. I can see why Random House felt compelled to add a disclaimer then, though I am certainly not in favour of that sort of thing. At least they didn't refuse to publish the book.

N-S: No, they didn't refuse to publish the book, but how they went about presenting it was certainly a telling prelude to the behind-the-scenes manipulations exerted on the literary establishment by the budding security state in the early days of the Cold War. It's impossible not to see a connection between the reception of *The Double Axe* and for instance the CIA's involvement in *Ramparts* magazine.

W: Returning to your comment on Glissant: is that what usually guides your decision to translate something, the desire to share what you think matters? Presumably there is some financial imperative behind a proportion of your translation work, too. How have you found balancing one concern against the other?

N-S: There are few better ways to share your love for certain texts than to translate them. While I have partly supported myself through my translation work, none of the books I've worked on have had a financial imperative to them. After all, these days, especially when I'm working on more marginalised authors from say North Africa or the Caribbean, most publishers won't even touch any of my manuscripts unless they come attached with some sort of grant and I've consistently turned down the chance to work on more commercial projects. I just couldn't bring myself to do it, partly because I knew I'd do a miserable job. Translation is all-consuming activity and if you're not in love with the manuscript and cannot see a link between that text and your own artistic sensibilities and directives, it would be too much of a slog. Making that call early on in my career proved to be a good decision. Most of the books I've translated fit into various themes I've attempted to tackle in my own work, for instance the interaction between the West and what it sees as its peripheral East and South, especially between Europe and Africa and the Middle East and how the spectre of imperialism still dominates that 'dialogue'. That's the running thread connecting most of my early translations.

W: What do you feel you accomplished during your three years at *Ambit*? How did this spirit manifest in that role?

N-S: I joined at a very exciting time. Barely a year into the job the magazine celebrated its 60th anniversary and thanks to an ACE grant, the first in its long run, we were able to tour the UK extensively, taking the magazine out of its habitual London cradle. Three years may sound like a long time, but this added up to eight issues (233–241). That said, I was beyond honoured to publish an excerpt from Yusef Komunyakaa's book-length poem, *The Last Bohemian of Avenue A*, an epic about life in NYC's Lower East Side, as well as Randall Horton's poems about his time in prison and Fred D'Aguiar's 'Burning Paradise', a mini-epic inspired by his experiences in a small town in Northern California destroyed by recent wildfires. I was also proud of one of the earliest poems I published, Julian Stannard's 'Eau Sauvage', partly inspired by Lord Lucan, the British peer who was accused of murder and vanished. Despite the darkness and gravity of the subject matter, I defy anyone to read that poem and not break out in hysterics. Stannard is one of our best and he isn't given enough credit, although the poem was long-listed for the Forward Prize for Best Single Poem. I was especially glad to publish younger poets such as Caleb Femi, Róisín Kelly, Jenny Xie, Threa Almontaser, Hibaq Osman, Taher Adel and Mona Kareem, as well as poets who will soon publish debut collections, including Supriya Kaur Dhaliwal and Gboyega Odubanjo. I also published poems from a dozen languages including Arabic, Polish, Spanish and Yiddish. Key to my work at *Ambit* were my efforts to change the magazine's editorial make-up – given that I was the first poetry editor of colour in the magazine's history – and I greatly expanded the roster of contributing editors, as well as hand-picking my successors, first Jade Cuttle, who left us for *The Times*, and then Romalyn Ante and Kostya Tsolakis.

W: What do you hope to bring to *Poetry London*? And what is there not enough of at present in the British poetry press, in your opinion?

N-S: Radical change is long overdue. What's missing? Empowerment. I'm not interested in 'diversity' and 'representation', trite bureaucratic buzzwords usually employed by those wishing to shore up their own jobs and positions of influence. 'Look', they tell you, 'I've filled my quota' and then they expect you to shut up and be content with whatever scraps they've thrown at you. Meanwhile, their clout and authority remain unchallenged, perpetuating disenfranchisement. Our prize culture deserves its fair share of the blame here, too. I've served on enough juries to know that the challenging, daring books seldom win. Here's what the average process looks like: Judge 1 picks Book A, Judge 2 picks Book B and so they settle on the usually mediocre Book C to avoid any protracted conflict, neither judge walking away satisfied. Then we're supposed to sit there and clap. Surely we can do better than that. We owe it to ourselves, and above all, to our readers and audiences. We should also look out for the way that 'diversity' is being used as

a cover to re-energise the domination of the upper classes on the artistic establishment, given that many of the poets of colour who are elevated by the establishment share a class affinity with the very people they are meant to replace. Many poets of colour will tell you they're tired of being used to shore up a magazine or institution's diversity ratings before eventually being shown the door and that they'd rather have *real* power, *real* jobs, *real* influence. This is why I've been very excited by the work done by Rachel Long's Octavia Collective, Naush Sabah and Suna Afshan's *Poetry Birmingham* and Nick Makoha's Obsidian Foundation, to name only a few. It's the only way forward.

W: What makes these different and exciting to you? What is 'the only way forward'?

N-S: What I mean is that enabling writers of colour to set up their own initiatives where they're not always being asked to justify their own approach will increase the range of participants from various backgrounds in the literary world. Many writers of colour don't often get to occupy senior editorial roles because many were locked out of the world of internships/work placements, the unique preserve of middle-class white kids whose parents happen to live in London, or who can afford to float them financially. The results are obvious. Only four major literary magazines currently have non-white editors in senior roles – Kayo Chingonyi at *The White Review*, Romalyn Ante at *Ambit*, Malachi McIntosh at *Wasafiri* and me. Change will be slow to come – after all, *PL* hired me as its first editor of colour after 33 years of being around – which is why it's necessary to have new publishing initiatives like *harana* (which first brought me into contact with Ante) and *Poetry Birmingham*. I don't think more magazines run by poets of colour will necessarily trigger a 'trickle-down-diversity' effect, but it's a start. I think the feeling of community is also important, ergo why I mentioned Octavia Collective. Obsidian, a one-week retreat for black poets led by black tutors, was clearly inspired by the US's Cave Canem Foundation and given the success of the latter, it's likely that it'll help nurture a generation of powerful voices.

W: You give a neat summary of the problem you see with how prizes are usually judged. And yes, surely we can do better. But what is the solution?

N-S: I think it's worth scrapping prizes altogether, although I'm certainly more fond of end-of-career prizes than any of the others. It somehow makes more sense, although by then most writers have stopped caring anyway. Many writers I've met – including winners of renowned prizes – understandably care more about the purse than the laurels. When Anna Burns was awarded the Man Booker prize in 2018, she said she'd be using the money to pay off her debts, which sounds about right. If all we care about is the money then what's the point? Given that there are various art funds handing out grants, what value should we really place on prizes? To help publicists shift more copies of our books? There are other – and less divisive – ways to do that. I'd also like to see a proper revival of serious review culture. So many excellent editors have had their pages cut and their hands tied and I think a certain presumptively woke political sensitivity also keeps us from discussing weighty issues without resorting to partisan platitudes and obtuse tribalism.

W: Your debut collection certainly discusses weighty issues, often in poetic reportage. I think, for example, of your montage of impressions of 'progress' in 'Home After Five Years', which ends with 'home' 'swelling like a cancer' below the departing plane. In 'Fidelity', you write 'I've seen too much. I shut my eyes and dive back / into the murky ocean of memory', and the third section of the book carries an epigraph from Antal Szerb: 'History is my only country'. To what extent is outrage at corporate greed and short-sightedness, and attendant public lassitude, a motivation for you, and does personal memory offer any salvation? Also, how have people reacted to your forthright portrayals of them in that book?

N-S: I wouldn't look to memory for salvation, but perhaps there's some redemption in acceptance. I'm working on that. *The Promised Land* is the notebook of my time in the UAE and above all it's a portrait of life in Abu Dhabi, a city I still love, despite it all. I took my family's travails as the book's not-so secondary subject, because I knew the lives of the UAE's forgotten migrants had to be recorded and elegised in some manner. My mother didn't particularly enjoy my frankness, but my brother did. It's tough to be written about and I tried to keep that in mind. The UAE is a federation of seven absolute monarchies – in the Louis XIV sense of the term – and they've gotten increasingly drunk on power: the genocide in Yemen, the colonisation of East Africa, the meddling in Syria, Egypt and Libya and the constant sabre-rattling with Iran, and that's just the tip of the iceberg. Writing that book was also partly a reaction to what I was often told in my early years coming up in London's literary world, namely that I was wasting my time writing about the UAE, because it was 'too ugly', or 'plastic', or 'soulless', etc. In part of the book I turned my lens towards British expatriates – the sort of people who read the *Guardian* and vote Labour at home, but who scream at their servants and nannies and spend their evenings whoring when they find themselves back in the familiar role of sahibs. Plenty of them live out Raj-era fantasies. After all, the UAE is governed by a strict, if unofficial racial caste system. There's a lot of anger in that book. The 'boom town' feel of the place produces a time warp that ultimately devastates the lives of the country's most vulnerable non-citizens. There's a reason they don't put clocks on the walls of casinos. It gets in the way of the house always winning. Call it poetic reportage, or docupoetry, but the idea of using poetry to discuss weighty issues has always fascinated me, quite likely inspired by my reading of Aimé Césaire's

Cahier d'un retour au pays natal (1939) and Cesare Pavese's *Lavorare Stanca* (1936), works that were absolutely central to my development, as well as Ed Sanders's *1968: A History in Verse* (1997) and *The Poetry and Life of Allen Ginsberg* (2000), which really fed my passion for historical dissection.

W: Your poetry has come with descriptive titles: your collection is subtitled 'Poems from Itinerant Life', and your recent pamphlet is *The Other Side of Nowhere*. The latter ends with 'found poems' that, as I noted in a review, shine sudden bursts of torchlight on a fragmented American past that might fruitfully be remembered. These poems also remove you, at least ostensibly, from the work. Does this indicate the direction of your next collection?

N-S: Many of those poems were written in the Summer of 2018, when I spent several months in Cochise county, the south-eastern corner of Arizona. This is not far north of Bisbee, an old copper mining town, the site of one of the most infamous episodes in American labour history, namely the Bisbee Deportation of 1917, when over 1,200 striking miners and their families were rounded up by deputised thugs under the direction of the local Phelps Dodge bosses – a company still in operation, under a different name – and herded into cattle cars at gunpoint and shipped off to New Mexico. My time there coincided with a commemoration honouring the dead and deported held on the 101st anniversary of the event and I was in attendance. I was briefly detained by the Border Patrol on my way out of Bisbee even though that was several miles north of the border. It's a history that needs to be remembered, but isn't. Some may know about the Battle of Blair Mountain (1921) and the Appalachian Coal Wars, but the West's equally bloody and troublesome history of racial and labour struggles are buried under several layers of oblivion. Many of the miners involved in those Western struggles were Native Americans and Mexicans, so they get less attention than the white-dominated labour struggles on the East Coast, where the African-American component also doesn't get its just dues. The pamphlet is dominated by these stories and the legacy of the First Red Scare, while the present rears its head through my efforts to discuss the so-called Mediterranean Migration Crisis, which should really be called the Great Drowning. The found poems were a means for me to let certain historical characters speak for themselves. None of them were poets, but you couldn't tell from the words they left behind. I was hesitant to speak for them. *The Other Side of Nowhere* proved to be the germ for my second collection, *High Desert*, which I've just completed. In many ways it's an ode to the American Southwest, from the city of Los Angeles to the rusting homesteads of Joshua Tree and the old copper mines of Arizona, charting the region's forgotten legacies of labour and racial struggles from the Spanish colonial period to the present day.

Two Poems

JORDI SARSANEDAS

translated by Stanley Moss

September

It neighs through small farms and hills.
September is the name of this horse.
See its eye
clear the sharp horizon,
ripen the mountains.
Its hair scatters sun-pollen
over red clay.

September is the name of this horse.
Up to the main square through the streets,
were today a holiday (it is not),
the people of the neighborhood would see it pass,
jobs know suddenly they become trees
in the peace of a high garden.

On balconies the palms of last Easter
are suddenly disheveled and silent clouds go galloping by.
Gallant crops of summer,
trail feathers
and Finch and Partridge,
a full flock of leaves
sweep the skin of the road,
whose cat jumps to a roof
and claws the shadows of leaves.

The sun whinnies.
The little horse
merry-go-round,
blond and black and round,
up and down,
down you come
one after one.

September,
now the night the most secret of lights.
The gust of grey sea on the window,
The gust of forests in the town.
Scandinavian long ships haul golden leaves
they will pulp to save and praise
their tree gods in winter.

Song of the Hack Driver

I have taken off my cap, crowned myself with flowers
and stop lights to inaugurate the street festival of liberty.

The good ghosts with drums went off-stage from the open,
a theory of theoretical spirits, a canticle
drowning in bubbles of carbonated water.

That last one stands in a formal garden,
between a laurel full of cats' eyes and a laurel full of communion veils,
forgotten, holding handfuls of veils
like Isadora Duncan.
The garden was black as the marrow of a bear.
She picked up the head;
the head was quite big, round.
Not completely round but well inflated
by the hair, of course.
It was a sun, big and red above the fall of Humpty Dumpty.
She was alone at the meadow's end
with the torch of liberty.
She put the head in a round basket
and 'plop' downs the lid (because this basket had a lid),
crossed her hands over the head of John the Baptist,
crossed her hands over the head of Julien Sorel.

Afterwards, sing joys of May and crops of June.
The May Queen, a girl fattened on Rosemary, Columbine,
and lustral water, who is sacrificed in May;
    Au joli mois de mai.

The harvests come with brown breasts,
no head so green that it does not ripen.
Yet, 'Come June, sickle in the fist,'
or, better said, sickle to the neck.

Heureux les epis murs et les bles moissones!
Yes, yes...
the round white disk of common ware
is piled high with red peaches
for my friends the painters.

Crossing her hands over the heads of John the Baptist
and Julien Sorel and their tranquility,
she sang of the returning sun
the infallible return of the sun.
'It's all for the best,'
and went off
with the head tidied up in the basket.
O mother I am in the happy belly of an ox
where it does not rain or snow.

Free hack, green light, green light, green.
Crowned with Roses, head uptown.

Language, Home and Threshold
Digging in Arabic and English
YOUSIF M. QASMIYEH

> Is language in possession, ever a possessing or possessed possession? Possessed or possessing in exclusive possession, like a piece of personal property? What of this being-at-home [*être-chez-soi*] in language toward which we never cease returning?
>
> — Derrida, *Le monolingualisme de l'autre: ou la prothèse d'origine*
> (*Monolingualism of the Other; or, The Prosthesis of Origin*)

I own no language. Departing from this premise, I begin with language in Arabic, treating it as a hinge through which insides and outsides are constantly reimagined in writing. In a way, I return to the non-existent home through language. In my case, the Arabic that is written into English takes place through articulations of what could be denominated as permanent traces in one's (mother) tongue. This is a recounting through language of a poetry that is continually in translation, the personal carried through time so as to be constructed in the future as thresholds, each threshold an instant where eyes can see one's arrival and departure.

Wreathed in vowels

I return to my mother tongue – the tongue of an illiterate mother. But is the return not an admission of a desertion in the first place? I reattach myself to sounds as sparse as a line of ants, hoping that my remembering who I am enables me to translate myself into language.

> a stranger *Wreathed in vowels*
> a stranger *A circumcised tongue*

I speak in two tongues. I write in two tongues. Not equally. Not with the ease of the native who is only existent in memory. I would say: Arabic and English are bartered in writing so as to see that what I speak is a possibility beyond itself. In poetry, the two shoulder my sins for me. The Arabic to my right, where senses equate to my impending off-balancedness as I drag the pen from right to left not knowing why it is that the right is right and the left is left. The English on the page, to the left, in ink, with silhouettes that look like inbuilt crosses from afar, as if the eyes are not themselves when they see. As if what is written to be pronounced (alive) is a memory of its sound.

It was through the acronym UNRWA, in my home camp, where I came across English – the English for those who cannot read English but can still see difference: from rations received seasonally bearing the letters U-N-R-W-A, from recycled school books doubly and triply sealed with those five letters. What is quite peculiar here is how an English acronym, which is supposed to be a representation and/or a deputisation of the absent words, metamorphosed into a fully-fledged Arabic word, written as one entity – rather than disparate bodies – and carrying a meaning in one language extracted from traces of another. Two languages sit side by side, the Arabic taking the English into my mouth through the spoon of the UN (United Nations). So, prodded by the perishable in what I was given, is the earliest English that would grow in my imagination, a survival pact came about between myself and the voice for a later life.

Now, in poetry, the Arabic and English occupy their times, with an eye to their coming time together, and what is to be inscribed next. They do so for the sustenance of a memory in progress or in anticipation of an inflow (with no detectable source to speak of) into a third time of their making. In poetry, I can sense language at the cusp of happening – in languages subscribed to their own life, but also open to plurality. For me, as a way of lessening the impact of such a moment, everything should return to translation: it is the one space that admits strangers as themselves. As translation is conversion (so Jacques Derrida tells us), strangers are converts, not only in text but also in the flesh. Loyal to the unknown, I only retain my name as two in languages.

From right to left, I turn to language, meandering through past homes with roofs constructed in haste from zinc and asbestos for the promise that above us one day would be concrete.

For it is a calf...

Before me, comes language. The one called upon whenever boredom befalls writing. In Arabic, *lugha* (language), has long grafted itself to generate what is beyond its means vis-à-vis what could be benevolently referred to as sense. In other words, the sounds in which people confide in order to speak sense are the same ones that bear their nonsensical correlative in the same setting. The inherent deficiency attributed to the way in which the word 'language' developed, both conceptually and linguistically is, one might argue, the trigger behind what it is that is a language. For it is what is known of language that is put to the test: in this sense, language becomes a shape, not only for itself but also for what is out there to be integrated within its folds.

Intriguingly, as its etymology vouches, it is the word *lugha* that ushers in the plural in imagination which in turn coalesces into more plurals with every suspicion of what it is that is a language. To repel the deficiencies of language or to constantly remember the deficient body of language that is, *is* to speak language. Indeed, it is this inherent deficiency in language that prompted the 10th-century Muslim scholar, Abū Manṣūr Al-Azharī (895–980 AD), to poignantly place *language* under the category of 'one of the deficient nouns' which journeys from another, presumably more complete and less popular, word: *lughwa* (morphologically larger than *lugha*). Premised on the above change, as language has evolved, instead of gaining more limbs to counter this self-inflicted incompleteness, it has in effect lost one more letter, the sound w, from *lughwa* to *lugha*. This historical contraction of the word, as Arab philologists advocate, is primarily to make the word 'language' more accessible to its utterers by virtue of shortening the distance between the mouth and the ear. Thus, by making the word less visible, language is made more accessible. This metamorphosis, from one feminine word to another, also consumes within it the journey that the meaning itself has undergone.

Take the following word, for example: derived from the same root, *laghā* is the (camel) calf that cannot be counted towards indemnity or blood money due to its insignificant stature and vulnerable age and therefore cannot be relied upon to outweigh the severity of what has been committed in the first place. Such corporeal and temporal facets inherent within language become even more discernible as soon as the somatic body of the word is taken into consideration, and the way in which proximity to meaning is so predisposed to the changes the word *lugha* itself has undergone in the first place. Let me explain: the word that is supposed to delimit meaning or, at minimum, establish a closer bond with what is considered meaning, has itself endured multiple alterations, including, in particular, semantic and morphological ones, in doing so rendering it *in the flesh* a true reflection of its substance. Indeed it is the assumption that speaking more than one tongue is, to quote Abdelfattah Kilito, 'to be on the right or on the left' of language itself.

Thresholds as/of the house and home

No one knows for certain whether the *ʾataba* (threshold) marks an entry or an exit; or whether what is peacefully assumed to be at the doorstep to welcome (or repel) is in fact a marker of an end. This is by no means a dialectic but rather a concrete reminder that for the threshold to be, the house should be there in advance. Traditionally made of wood, the threshold embodies the borderline: as one enters the private, one simultaneously exits the public and vice versa. It is also a holy site frequented by worshippers desperate to be blessed by the revered dead. In my case, it is an integral part of me. A divider that sits exactly at the heart of things. The motif prompting one imagination at the expense of another. A constant deliberation in the event of writing (in language)

between one language and another. Is it not the case that a threshold denotes the non-existent before the existent?

Under the impression of making something to protect our UN-gifted place, my father made us a threshold. In my home camp, at the entrance of a house made of hollow bricks, my father erected his threshold. This time made of concrete. Pure cement to withstand God and time. That was the threshold, the one built, stroked and seasonally expanded by the father until it devoured the house. For us, the threshold came to signify our ownership of a place that was not ours but a pending one for some other time that might be remembered – when allowed enough time – at some different times in a *threshold-less* camp. To guard the threshold before the house, my father, like a craftsman, would thicken the threshold with extra layers of cement, intimately touching the main door overlooking the alleyway in our camp. With our and the neighbours' thresholds expanding, leading to a continual contraction in time and space, images – accumulated between the house and the threshold – would gradually seep through. Like a *ṭalal* (ruin) to those who traverse it, the threshold invites me over like a *Jahili* poet, now in two languages, both at the threshold, not to lament the lost house or the untraceable traces of those who are no longer in the place but rather to retain a time whose sight is through the excess of a house. Language, for me, will always be at the threshold, where animals are sacrificed so proximity between imagination and the written is bridged.

Interiority returns to *home* or at minimum to what is considered one. In this tentativeness lies *home*. Resonating with English, and in line with the Greek source, the word *ʾistiʿāra* (metaphor) in Arabic is predicated on borrowing what is not within the means of the borrower. In borrowing, the image is instantly transferred from one place to another, in effect established as a new status (quo), where a new owner is to be announced, albeit impermanently. So the transferral enacted in images changing hands is where the metaphor is, a home which is subject to what is taken; above all what is taken is repeated afresh, or deconstructed and reconstructed from scratch.

The midwife in the camp would always sit on the threshold of her home. Wrapped in white, a diminutive figure, spectral, with hands more visible than her body. She would eat sunflower seeds and throw the shells to the would-be archivists and those who dwell on meaning, or the lack thereof, of yet another day. As we say dialectally, the *qaṣqaṣa* (the munching of seeds by separating the shell from the edible), grounded in *qi qiṣṣa* (story), is what keeps us alive as we monitor the passing before us with an ear to the tale and an eye on people and things. The midwife: the witness, at the threshold, to birth, birthing and death. I recoil, my language tucked in my heart, to remind myself that I speak the tongue with which I was born and the one to come.

I talk in translation. I talk in language.

From underneath my mother's veil, the shape of a square, stretched from all angles to cover her hair *(sha'r)* and my poetry *(shi'r)* for they (hair and poetry) in Arabic are the mirror image of each other without diacritics!

Beneath the hair, above the headscarf, is a place
The ever-expanding threshold
Signatures, fingerprints, contracts, bodily avowals.

In Baddawi camp, my family's home comprised two houses, the one allocated to my grandmother and her family and the one which was assigned later, adjacent to my grandmother's, to my father as a newly-married man, both gifted to us by the United Nations. Basic builds. Soft brick walls. Cemented floors. Roofs made of zinc first, then asbestos. Despite the gradual disappearance of the borders that once separated my grandmother's from my father's, the old wall remains, with remnants of historical clay that were kept by my father as a *talal* (ruin) to bear witness to a historical rupture between the mother and the son but equally to how a home is constantly reconfigured from within to give the impression of an imagined other.

As vast as a verse is my home

'For our house is our corner of the world,' writes Gaston Bachelard. Retreating to a place happens in reality when the place itself is reachable, not only materially but within the written as well. To inscribe the house in language necessitates intimate engagement with the house's constituents but above all with its multiple written meanings. For me, as someone whose house is never within reach to begin with – as the *mine-ness* of possession normally carried in the English language was in fact solely a temporary gift from the United Nations to my family, it is what is written for this place that reattaches me to a place in language. And here I am, talking about Arabic and English, two languages I grapple with while grappling with the discreet in the poetic in both writing and translation. But before I sign this pact with what is not mine topographically, strictly speaking, though given access to wander within its parameters, let me return to my first encounters with what house (also home) is.

'[A] privileged entity' is the house, Bachelard contends, where its accessibility bifurcates innumerable sensibilities and sensitivities. In Arabic, also, *bayt* is not merely a word. It is in essence a contract between the occupants and the place for neither party to relinquish the other until the day comes. Where one rests is where one rests completely. This is the Arabic premise as inferred from what a *bayt* is. That is why it is classically taken to mean the home and the tomb. You live, and you die, in the place. The three letters *b-y-t* (with the muted middle sound) resemble a *middleness* that is all-encompassing, where all gravitates to the middle. Within the muted middle lies the dweller and the dead in the very same spot. I write *bayt* into my poetry as though it were the pending tomb, a deferred time that I am now living in retrospect. But when I translate *bayt* into English, I render it as benignly as possible for the sake of holding on to the secrets of a language that I claim to be mine. I render it as a bare place, with no afterlives to revert to,

and no time to carry it across newer times. An unsuspicious word, innocuous for my own survival as a stranger who speaks in two cracked tongues. Not because injecting the English with the Arabic is impossible or transferring literality across them is unachievable, but because re-enacting with exactness can deprive language of its own air – the air needed for the inside in particular. *Contra* Bachelard's house as 'a vertical being', *bayt* submits to the horizontality of discreteness; in essence, to living and dying discreetly. In this case, imagination belongs to the house's interiority, more so than to that which exists beyond the house. For the *bayt* to be sustainable as a place of refuge, its innards automatically become bigger for the now-time and hereafter. Perhaps that is why, in referring to mosques as *buyūt Allah* (houses of God), *buyūt* being one of the plural forms of *bayt*, this new construction, structural but also genitive through the bond between *bayt* and Allah, ordinary houses are displaced in favour of divine ones.

The poetic verse is also called *bayt*. Classically segmented into two parts, two halves on the same line separated by a void so they maintain distance and time. A linear structure, as is referred to, gradually beckoning the vertical poem as verses are piled upon verses. But why *bayt*? Herein words are hosted within what will be the same body in the future, amassed according to strict schemes so that wondrous worlds are pondered by the poet-constructor. Plurally, they are *abyāt*, to distinguish them from the ordinary houses, *buyūt*. In this, composing a poem harbours a translation, a movement, from the stable in the house to another human condition where homes are *concretely* formed in words. Whether in Arabic or in English, such a conversion, from home as a thought and materiality to a home in words whereby individuality is retained, interpreted and reinterpreted, cannot but be a new itinerary to newer homes. Irrespective of how *home* is conceived of, it always belongs to its interiority, as a matter of survival beyond the visible. To build a house is to wonder what interiority is before undertaking the act of building, where walls are going to be erected, what corners will take shape, and above all in what language, or languages, all of this (in the future) will be imagined.

In the corner I sat. The holy corner, they said, before vanishing into thin air. The words clanked like rusty locks in empty pails. In the opposite corner, the imam sat, cross-legged, ghostly save his eyes, reciting the *Cow Chapter*, verse dovetailing another verse, sounds collapsing at the threshold, eternal humming, while I continued screaming for my mother and her grasp.

The corner, not the one in the house, but the *zāwiya* or *rukn*, in places devoted to recitation and the needy, a place encroaching on another place until it is no longer a place but a remnant of it. Too narrow, so it is a cognate with solitude. To render the plural one in their isolation. Or, to imagine voices, noises and languages collapsing into the same pot, not knowing which is which, not knowing whose language it is that is reaching God.

As it is the written that stays behind, I write for myself: poetry as translation and translation as poetry. Taught to speak in dialect, I pronounced what I heard, never as things that were, but as a supplement to what a dialect would be one day, free of shibboleths, with a place for an other as he is. Through dialect, rehearsing is what I have been doing for a long time, for a second tongue where mispronunciation is the law and where meaning is susceptible to (and suspicious of) all places we call home, thresholds and corners. To be suspicious in writing is to write memory anew as though it had never existed. It is in meaning (according to its Arabic pattern, the word *maʾna* – meaning – is technically a place!) where language and place meet as a filiation that knows no stasis. For they are attuned to the specificity of strangeness, I will repeat Derrida's words:

Everything is summoned from an intonation.

Absolutely everything, including how we pronounce our places into writing.

Reviews

The Utility of Happiness

American Originality, Louise Glück
(Carcanet) £14.99
Reviewed by Valerie Duff-Strautmann

Louise Glück, American author of
twelve books of poetry, won the
Nobel Prize for literature in 2020.
This honour was bestowed not only
for books of poems but also for two
collections of essays: *Proofs & Theo-
ries* (1994) and *American Originality*
(2017). Over the last half century,
beginning with *Firstborn*, Glück's
books of poems have been pub-
lished at intervals ranging from
seven to two years, garnering much
attention (including a Pulitzer for
The Wild Iris); the two books of
essays saw a gulf of over twenty
years between them, despite
acclaim for *Proofs & Theories,* which
won the PEN/Martha Albrand award.
What does *American Originality* offer,
following so late on the heels of
Proofs?

There's notable similarity
between these books; in both, one
hears Glück discussing poetry as if
to a group of fortunate students
(she has been teaching poets almost
as long as she's been publishing).
'American Narcissism', 'Ersatz
Thought', 'On Buddenbrooks', and
'American Originality' – the essays of
Part One, academic even in title,
each take the shape of a well-
wrought lecture as Glück builds her
thought and anticipates questions.
These essays draw from a wealth of
experience in the field – for example,
in 'On Originality':

> Under the brazen 'I made up a
> self' of the American myth, the
> sinister sotto voce, 'I am a lie.' [...]
> The literary art of our time mirrors
> the invented man's anxiety; it also
> affirms it. You are a fraud, it seems
> to say. You don't even know how to
> read. And for writers, this curious
> incomprehension, this being
> ahead of the time, linked as it is
> to affirmation, seems superficially
> encouraging, as though 'to
> understand' meant 'to exhaust'.

Or in 'American Narcissism', which
follows a range of writers from Dickin-
son and Whitman to the present day:

> Dickinson introduces a type of
> veiled disclosure that will found

whole schools of poetry, disclosure
so charged, so encoded, so intent
on limited selective revelation as
to privilege the reader. Dickinson
isn't narcissistic because the other
postulated by the poems cannot,
in its function, become an aspect
of the self, though this is exactly,
I believe, what happens later.

One finds similar explorations in Part
Two, but 'Story Tellers', 'On Realism',
and 'The Culture of Healing' hover
in the world of late twentieth/early
twenty-first century poetry. Her con-
temporary preferences surface here.
'Story Tellers', for example, examines
the work of Robert Pinsky and Ste-
phen Dobyns, Glück's peers. The
reader is expected to have some famil-
iarity with these two American poets
at this level of discourse, and if they
do, through her discussion of their
bodies of work, she solidifies what
is otherwise an unexpected pairing.
'Even at the level of grammar, the
single fascination Dobyns shares with
Pinsky, a fascination with cause and
effect,' Glück observes, connects these
two poets of 'relentless mobility'.

Part Three, or 'Ten Introductions',
is where *American Originals* and
Proofs & Theories part ways (although
Proofs did include her general intro-
duction to the 1993 edition of *Best
American Poetry*). For many years,
Glück judged prestigious first book

contests; this section is a collection of introductions to the winning books. Each one says much about her aesthetic and range, revealing what an 'original' might look like. Describing her purpose as judge, Glück writes: 'I was reading to fall in love: panning for gold was how I saw it... The introduction, which I had feared, was thrilling to write. I felt I had discovered an immense talent; the act of describing it took on a genuine urgency, not unrelated to messianic fervor.'

The book could have ended there, but she ends with a nod to *Proofs & Theories,* returning to her own life experiences as subject. In several essays in *Proofs*, we watch an adult looking back, making sense of how she became the person and writer she is. In the final essay of *American Originality*, Glück looks back on a lifetime of writing and choices. She ends imparting permission to others:

And although no one can guarantee that the married doctor with children will also write enduring poetry, or that the passionate adolescent who finally permits himself maturity and pleasure will evolve into a deeper thinker, the person who, through cautious clinging to the known, the ostensibly safe, arrests or constrains his native fascination with medicine or desire for family is diminishing the possibility of his making original art. Meaning art unique to a specific and profoundly lived experience... Let me urge now the utility of happiness.

Kissing tenderly

Snow Approaching on the Hudson, August Kleinzahler (Faber) £10.99
Reviewed by Nuash Sabah

In a poem toward the end of August Kleinzahler's new collection, an admiring young driver – presumably tasked with collecting the poet for an event – interrogates him: '*he* was determined, all right // to find out what, I could not surmise. About how / I went about stringing these words together, as I do, / or some clue to be found in my speech patterns or facial gestures?' The interlocutor goes on to ask what seems a pious question about whether Kleinzahler is corporate, an idea that's malaxated in the poem into a curious absurdity. I completely understood the driver's enthusiastic probing, however: Kleinzahler is a virtuosic alchemist with language, and a knowing one at that. He ends the poem, 'And I did like his car, an '87 Signature Series Lincoln Town Car, / 6-way power seats and blue carriage roof. It handled like a dream...'

Stacked modifiers and specific, sometimes technical, often catalogic descriptions are characteristic – there's an indulgent description of a Citroën C4 in the second poem of the book – but what's more interesting is how technology, nature, and human geography cohabit seamlessly in the poet's imagination and are treated with the same musical, luxuriating attention to detail. The title poem first struck me as one of few in the collection with shorter lines, a more clipped lyric and form, but it is an example of Kleinzahler at home on the Hudson, the lingering presence of mist and cloud, the image of a 'giant HD plasma screen... flashing red and green' up next to the 'stamped seal in a Sesshu broken ink scroll', movement in the sky and on the river; 'bustle of traffic in the sky, here, as well, on the shore below'. Implicit too in the poem is the effect of light, another recurring theme, here obscured by mist but elsewhere in the collection it's 'pearly' or 'electric with pinks and reds' (not neon signs, but a description of clouds at sunset over the Hudson).

This is a book of personae and polyphony; Kleinzahler continues his sequences 'Traveler's Tales' and 'A History of Western Music', with poems titled as numbered chapters in these ongoing series. Previous instalments have appeared in earlier collections and in the *London Review*

of Books and the poems are voiced by historical or imagined characters, though some are in the poet's voice, such as 'A History of Western Music: Chapter 42', which is addressed to the late William Corbett, a friend and the interviewer in Kleinzahler's *Paris Review* interview. His own voice strikes the note of a wistful storyteller, keenly perceptive, witty, nostalgic – though in a frank and clear-sighted sort of way – and the voices of his characters are fully realised and distinct from the first line:

A quandry, to be sure: kissing, / tenderly, hungrily atop the bluff on a greensward off Boulevard East, / right by the steps of the Old Grauert Causeway, winding down / to the waterfront far below, the Hopper painting, two streets south / on 49th. He must have climbed up all those steps, sketchbook in hand. / She was luscious, my word, was she ever, dark as a Moor and filled with ardor – / for me, if you can imagine. Who can say why? We had only just met, / in the corner of a nearby bar and were almost immediately hard at it.

This from 'East Wind over Weehawken', a startling ekphrastic poem, and 'Chauncy Hare' is another, where the work of an artist is briefly reimagined through the narrative of a character who might exist in its world. Kleinzahler poems thrust the reader into their stories and locations, and the sheer breadth of both in the collection is dizzying; we move from Canada, across America, to Europe and beyond. His subject matter too is as varied as his cast of characters; we encounter a colony of ants at war (in perhaps my favourite poem of the collection), an Italian filmmaker, a Greek shipping magnate, couples on holiday in Istanbul or Paris, a long list of Joneses, a homeless 'Shadow Man', an errant women's soccer coach, an old flame looking for an agent... This smorgasbord of a collection displays not only facility across registers, with diction and voice, a poet who's a masterful technician, but also one who is deeply curious about the world and able to transmute that curiosity into vivid, satisfying storytelling that moves fast but unlocks slowly for the reader – Chambers and Google may be welcome friends.

Wicked Enchantment

Wicked Enchantment, Wanda Coleman, ed. Terrance Hayes (Penguin) £9.99
Reviewed by Rommi Smith

Wicked Enchantment is the first publication of Wanda Coleman's poetry in Britain.

With the Guggenheim Fellowship, an Emmy and the 2012 Poetry Society of America's Shelley Memorial Award amongst her honours, Coleman was a prolific writer, authoring thirteen books of poetry, alone, during her lifetime. This volume – with its themes including police hassle, hustle, poverty, social invisibility, misogynoir and anti-Black racism – is published eight years after her death in 2013 (the same year the Black Lives Matter movement was founded). There are poems written after Black Panther co-founder, Huey P. Newton ('American Sonnet 16', p.128), and in memoriam of Emmett Till, the fourteen-year-old murdered by white supremacists in 1955, and whose murder is one of the inciting incidents of the modern Black American civil rights movement. There is a bittersweet sense of justice in reading this book: it should earn Coleman the title of the official Black Lives Matter Poet Laureate, posthumously.

Perhaps Wicked Enchantment will bring the author the international recognition which eluded her in her lifetime. That missing impact during her life had already led Camille Paglia to declare: 'she's not as central as she should be, her language jumps off the page' and scholar Jennifer Ryan to write, in 2015: '[h]er sudden absence from a literary landscape that never fully recognised her particular ingenuity, coupled with the breadth and complexity of her work, signify that now is the time for a major assessment of her oeuvre.' Wicked Enchantment is part of that 'major assessment'.

As this selection demonstrates, Coleman's devotional practice, as a poet, was in centring narratives erased by prejudice and privilege and challenging the establishment. In 'Beaches, Why I Don't Care for Them' (pp.14–15) which, in part, concerns how American beach culture (as metaphor for American culture) is hostile to Blackness and Black bodies, Coleman casts herself as the 'feminist ahab stalking the great white whale.' In 'Doing Battle with the Wolf', Coleman's ink-tivism synonymises prejudice and poverty, in turn anthropomorphising them into the lone white wolf which 'howls' and 'scratches' at the door to her home:

> armed with my spear, inherited
>   from my father as he
> from his mother (who was
>   psychic) as she from her father
> (who was a runaway slave) as he
>   from his mother (who
> married a tribal witch doctor) –
>   me – african warrior
> imprisoned inside my female form
>   [...]

The author relishes language as inheritance and, indeed, lineage. Her hereditary 'spear' is reminiscent of Seamus Heaney's pen-as-spade in his poem Digging. Writing back is resistance – a craft of making oneself and one's people visible. Indeed, fear of invisibility is a trope in this book. In Sessions (pp.10–11), Coleman's narrator vents fury at a mercurial 'doctor' figure regarding her 'absence from the nation's tomes'. In 'Wanda in Worryland' (pp.3–4) Coleman writes: 'I get scared sometimes / and have to go look in the mirror to check if I'm / still here'. Her strategic lineation means the poem lands on a deft, two-syllable, defiant rebuttal to erasure; a compressed slogan worthy of emblazonment on protest sandwich boards and placards. Coleman honed a poetics of polymathy and curiosity; expansive stances against forces of limitation and oppression. She self-defined her practice as, 'a style composed of styles sometimes waxing traditional, harking to the neoformalists, but most of my poems are written in a sometimes frenetic, sometimes lyrical free verse, dotted with literary, musical and cinematic allusions, accented with smatterings of German, Latin, Spanish and Yiddish, and neologisms, and rife with various cants and jargons, as they capture my interest, from the corporate roundtables to the streets (xi).'

This capacious, expansive, shape-shifting, eclectic, abundant, multi-directional, fusive self-definition of her creativity, is best evidenced by Coleman, not solely in her 'sometimes lyrical free verse', but in her sonnets. Thirty-five of the sonnets (from her one-hundred-poem American Sonnets series) feature in this selected works. Those sonnets are a pyrotechnic display of dazzle, dirt, desire and downlow; experiments in lineation, case and punctuation – these latter elements hallmarks of post-Black Arts literary protagonists. Coleman shakes the sonnet free from any cosy stereotypes; taking on the form – and challenging its rules at the same time. Sound play, experimentation, refrain and call and response – definers of jazz and blues – are the root-notes of her sonnets, which range from the epistolary to the sensuous syntax of the sultry in 'American Sonnet 26': 'too nice too sincere too there. but lovemonger – / without you this city is a pale rude fiction. [...]' The reverberation of feeling for this sonnet's absent 'sweetsistuh goodheart' can be felt, not just in the volta of the tenth-line (which ends on the word 'rubyfruit') but across the whole body of the poem. It culminates (or climaxes?) on a charged couplet: 'along this parched desert floor where devil-tongues / ache for the magic rush of your angelgush'.

These are poems of orientation as much as disorientation; Coleman crafted them full of unrest as much as fabulation and fabulousness. In Wicked Enchantment here Coleman is: alive in word, pushing poetics forward whilst, Sankofa-style, looking back; as relevant to the present tense as to the past.

'My holy of holies'

Summer Snow, Robert Haas
(Ecco) $16.99
Reviewed by Tony Roberts

With Robert Hass's substantial new collection, *Summer Snow* – his first in a decade – we are again in the persuasive company of 'a virtuoso of common American speech' (as the *New York Times* recently described him). In his conversational way, Hass mulls over a lifetime's preoccupations: the ecology of his native Northern California; meditations on love and loss; political and eco-activism; the serendipities of language and the simple life.

Ever since *Field Guide* (1973) Hass has devoted himself to admiring and naming: flora, fauna, colours, tastes. He is the poet as guide: reverent, informative and good-humoured. 'Stanzas for a Sierra Morning', which adorns the back of the book, is characteristically descriptive, beginning with a search for wildflowers and ending – as an allegory of the creative act – in some exotic market, 'sipping tea, / An eye out for that scrap of immaculate azure' that is the blue of the sky.

The title *Summer Snow* alludes to the confusion of seasons in foggy Northern California and reawakenings. While Hass and his poet-wife, Brenda Hillman, are regularly drawn by the need to commune with nature ('you among buckbrush and huckleberry oak with the field guide in hand naming the lichens') other responsibilities intrude and redirect their attention. 'It's brutal, the way some lives / Seem to work and some don't', he writes in bewilderment at the sometimes suddenness of mortality.

'Harvest: Those Who Die Early in Their Middle Years' is one of a number of poems which deal with instances of death in the Seven Ages. It begins with the sound of Osaka peasants harvesting barley, which leads Hass to remember those friends cut down ('All of them suddenly become the work / they managed to get done'). It turns out that it is Buson, not Hass, who witnesses the harvest while thinking of his master Bashō's experience. This leads to Bashō's death poem, Ronald Blythe's translation, Whitman and finally Tennyson out walking, hearing barley reapers. Digressions typically come full circle.

If the early part of the book is concerned with untimely death, Hass later turns to murder. The dangers inherent in the politics of the American 'imperium' are scrutinised in 'The Creech Notebook', an involving autobiographical account of protesting outside Creech Air Force Base, home of military drones. 'Seoul Notebook' describes a peace conference, while 'After Xue Di' offers thoughts on 'asymmetrical warfare' and moral resignation. 'Dancing' begins with a satirical note on the American way: 'The radio clicks on – it's poor swollen America, / Up already and busy selling the exhausting obligation / Of happiness'; then moves immediately to its subjects: man's eternal fascination with violence; European and American imperialism and their progeny, the fanatical killers among us.

Summer Snow is not primarily a depressing collection, however. Hass is too sociable, too enthusiastic and too much the raconteur. He has an amusing story of an alligator and a ring, a Shakespearean anecdote about meeting a slaughterhouse worker on the Southern Pacific, and a delightful grandfather's eco tale. He loves to take off from something a friend has told him, or from hearing a life story, or imagining one. Hass will even venture *into* an allusion. One of the best poems –shocking and erotic –creates a conversation with his friend, Czesław Miłosz. Miłosz is one of the many literary figures mentioned in the collection, a number of whom crowd lasciviously into the droll, 'What the Modernists Wrote About: An Informal Survey'.

In his empathy and social activism, Hass follows in the tradition of critical compassion he so admires in Chekhov: '"My holy of holies,"' Chekhov, a doctor, wrote when he was asked about his religious and political convictions, "is the human body"' ('After Xue Di').

Skirting Melodrama

The Structure of Days Out, Tom Lowenstein (Shearsman) £16.95
Reviewed by Marius Kociejowski

Tom Lowenstein, poet and ethnographer, is now in his ninth decade and yet still he lingers in the margins of the literary scene. If there is justice enough, he will be brought to its centre. His most recent book, the fourth title in a series about the Alaskan Inupiaq, *The Structure of Days Out* is the most personal. A journal, augmented in places, it recounts his time spent in the village of Point Hope or Tikiġaq in the 1970s. The book goes over and beyond any interest one might have in the region and its people, so by the time we reach its penultimate chapter 'The House of Time' it becomes, perhaps unwittingly, a lively skeleton of the writer's credo. A work both haunting and haunted, it focuses on the lives of three people; a tribal elder called Asatchaq whom the author plies with Big Macs for his memories of the past; 'a high-toned old Christian woman' called Mrs Charlotte who as a young girl witnessed, in 1889, the aftermath of the Wounded Knee massacre; and, briefly but devastatingly so, a rambunctious young Tikiġaq woman called Daisy. Only a few pages are devoted to her, but she is the book's presiding spirit, alas. What happens to those who are caught between a near-forgotten past and the rotting ice floe that is the future?

The most fun is Mrs Charlotte. When Lowenstein met her in 1975 she was close to 100 years of age. She, not the author, describes herself in the words of Wallace Stevens's poem-title. She cites 'the incontinent old

Whitman ('There ain't no Jews in Whitman's America'), Milton, Keats, Marvell, *Rev. T.S. Eliot* ('*After Strange Gods,*' she cries. 'Mine-a-geedy, what a farrago! What pietistic nonsense!'), Edith Piaf, Rilke, Heinrich Heine (in German) and Kafka whose books she claims to have studied at university. There is a slight chronological muddle here because it would seem she knew Kafka's works *before* he had a chance to write them. It hardly matters and indeed her occasionally weak memory (or is it partly Lowenstein's?) greatly enhances what would make a tremendous adaptation for the stage. What in God's name is she doing there? Well, God knows. She went there as the wife of an Episcopalian preacher and after he died stayed on. A study in unlikelihood, she is the very epitome of those who end up in odd places.

The central figure is the elderly Asatchaq whom modernity has reduced to an internal exile. We last encounter him in a scene of unbearable pathos. An elderly man pushes over the rough ground a cooker on a piece of cardboard towards his cabin which has not the wherewithal to connect it. Lowenstein summons Shakespeare.

Was this, I wondered, put on for an audience? I don't think so, but remembered Malvolio rushing out in fury – or at least in the spectacle of one. Silence followed. Or was this Lear, storm-bound outwardly? Inwardly determined. Or Prospero dictating with his staff an end that would conclude politically? None of this, to Asatchaq, was tragic. It was just what happened.

A single observation sparks some of the most thoughtful passages in a book already full of wonders. Also it serves to bring together the many strands in the book, whose sum may be seen as the short change with which an ancient culture is left high and dry. The young have little time for Asatchaq's stories.

What was the meaning of these months of recitation? I hope I'm not wrong that the stories gave the old man pleasure. Pleasure is complex, involving a feeling of rightness, the happiness of

identifying with the appropriate, even an illusory sense of permanence, though the actual sensation of pleasure is usually fleeting. Yes: Asatchaq was putting something in place and I offered him the confidence that was his effort was worthwhile and would last. His pleasure was, moreover, allied to mine. He was filling a need: a demand from the past to bring the ancestral world back and substantiate a reality that otherwise would be lost and that he would lose touch with.

Lowenstein is too shrewd, though, to be lured into a romantic vision of the past as to go that way would be to belittle the lives of those whom he meets. 'It would be easy to look back and construct an historical melodrama,' he writes. 'There would be truth in such a scenario though I'd be embarrassed to render its dramatic significance.' Those are the words of a man humble enough to know hugely his place.

The Failure of the Moment

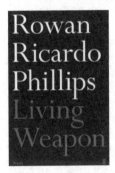

Living Weapon, Rowan Ricardo Phillips (Faber) £10.99
Reviewed by Kate Caoimhe Arthur

Should poetry respond to current crises, or is its job always best practised in the long gaze backwards? It is a surprise to find here poems about coronavirus bereavement ('Prelude'), the death of George Floyd ('Screens'), and Brexit (number three of the 'Trinidadian Triptych'). But the third installation of Rowan Ricardo Phillips's trilogy (preceded by *The Ground* (2012) and *Heaven* (2015) is in conversation with a vast cast of historic forebears who enliven Phillips's examination of the meaning, morality and musicality of

poetry, his 'living weapon'. Wordsworth, Donne, Heaney, Elizabeth Bishop, Arvo Pärt, Orpheus and Milton all step in to commend, argue with or bear witness to Phillips's meditations, and he is an eloquent and persuasive converser.

At the heart of the collection, and among its most delicious mouthfuls, is a scattering of sonnets. They display deft sonic footwork: rhyme is repeated and modulated by the gear-change of internal vowel-sounds, sending the poem off in a subtly different direction. '[T]he first fissions / Finally arriving at the listener, / Who makes sense of it sooner or later' ('The Peacock'). 'Night of the Election' describes the moment in the 2016 American election when 'A sad irrelevance [was] now relevant' and its immediate effect on language: 'The words became a thing looked at, not read.' He invokes 'Seamus Heaney's poem', at first assumed to be 'The Cure at Troy'; the failure of the moment is the failure to make hope and history rhyme. Instead:

In the poems place an oyster
Appeared on a plate: languid, the colour
Of vanilla, moist fennel, raw silver,
Crushed hay, sunk ships, quince and Jupiter.

Heaney's own 'Oysters' is invoked, in which he is 'angry that my trust could not repose/In the clear light, like poetry or freedom' and which ends with his desire to be 'verb, pure verb'.

This is also Phillips's purpose in language, and poetry is a 'living weapon'. Luminous, moving, the poem makes a claim for the value of poetry in dangerous times. The collection is at its best here, but memorable moments are also to be found in 'Spiegel im Spiegel': 'I swept away the heaps of broken glass/But I don't know where they went after that.' It's a weapon to be used in self-defence, as in 'Mortality Ode' in which the observational power of the cell phone is wielded in the moment of threat, when four police officers enter the phone repair shop in which the speaker waits. 'I open my phone's camera/To sneak a picture of them/Because it's four cops in a cell phone store'. The description of the secretive and roundabout way of capturing them on camera without causing fear and inciting violence, has something to say about the circumlocutions poetic language take in capturing its subject and making it the speaker.

The collection is bookended by two long prose poems; the first, '1776', describes the view of New York from the top of the Freedom tower, and the descent to the ground of a winged creature who observes the city in its resting moments, when a murmuration of starlings can be watched, for example. It is not immediately obvious that they are poems, Phillips is a respected non-fiction writer. The concluding prose poem, 'Portrait', is also a loving observation of a city, this time Barcelona, in peregrinations from the familiar tourist spots to the outskirts. As Jeremy Noel-Tod admits, the simplest definition of a prose poem is 'a poem without line breaks' and Phillips claims in an interview that he wanted to see how far he could push poetic form. It is not an experiment that worked for me, although there are moments of engaging tempo. 'The taxi is all mine now. I roll my window down' – which, it should be noted, uses a line break for effect. 'Flight is like untying the air itself, fold after fold and layer after layer'. These poems left me longing for the lyric that could still be in there.

Wisdom Literature

Infinity Diary, Cyril Wong
(Seagull Books) £16.99
Reviewed by Jee Leong Koh

Cyril Wong's first book release in the UK and the US invites reflection on his distinguished body of work. In addition to a volume of stories and two novels, Wong has written fourteen books of poetry, two of which won the Singapore Literature Prize. He is forty-three years old.

Infinity Diary, published by Calcutta-based Seagull Books, is a distillation of years of spiritual searching, away from childhood's homophobic Catholicism towards an adult tussle with Buddhist detachment. The search has been conducted through rigorous self-examination, writing daily. Hence the many books. Not all of them reach the same level of achievement, but the quality is consistently high. The main reason, as I see it, is that Wong does not lose sight of all the tunneling forces that sap spiritual life. The writing is urgent, because, like Wong's practice of meditation, it enacts 'rituals of survival' ('Between Infinity and You'). *Infinity Diary* is programmatic (a fearful word!) in that it offers a living program, the poet himself.

Formally, the spiritual agenda manifests itself in the use of the sentence as the main unit of sense and music. In his earlier work, Wong has shown himself a master of the line break, most thrillingly and subtly in his book-length poem *Satori Blues*. He understands what he calls in *Infinity Diary* 'the art of hope in the torque / of a line'. The love lyrics in this book are as tender and erotic as the Song of Songs, but they do not represent Wong's improvement on previous collections. Instead, the sentence, singly and in paragraphs, searches for an eloquent plainness. It embodies the poet's repeated injunction to himself and others to 'carry on' in spite of the distractions of decay and desire ('Every morning, old ladies tread carefully between their flats and the market, keeping death from spilling from their bodies.').

Sharply critical of 'millennials' who 'bloat their novels and jostle for international agents', Wong champions writers without literary pretensions who reveal truths encountered in the course of living. One such writer he highlights here is Bonny Hicks, a fashion model, whose autobiography *Excuse Me, Are You a Model?* (1990) outraged the morality police for its frank discussion of sexuality. In 'Plainspeak: Holes, Lines, Bonny Hicks', Wong quotes Hicks liberally for the resonance of her sentences, such as 'Health is merely the slowest possible rate at which one can die.'

Infinity Diary returns over and over again to embodied truths. In 'Vakkali Refractions', the story is retold of the disciple Vakkali who loves the Buddha for his physical beauty. For this impure love, the Buddha orders Vakkali to leave him and the Sangha. In the poet's own prose commentary on the story, he suggests that the Buddha's order is not rejection so much as necessary guidance for this monk, who must transcend his love of mere physical form. The poet-commentator asks, 'what is transcendence when there is nothing to transcend?' Instead of rejecting the corporeal, we should 'love our bodies and where they take us'. In the story of Vakkali, the distraught disciple throws himself over a cliff, but is saved by a few words from the Buddha and walks safely on air.

Wisdom literature is not all one reassuring note. Yes, it calls for salvation for one's people, but, like the Psalmist, it also calls for destruction on one's enemies. Wong takes bigoted straight people to task in the poem named for them, 'Dear Stupid Straight People'. He plots vengeance on homophobes: 'I hope your children grow up queer; I hope they write poems about you.' Internalised homophobia is not spared the withering scorn: 'To those of you proud of being "bisexual" or "post-homosexual" – please.'

Wong would be the first to confess that he is no Buddha. He enjoys hating too much. He is not a 'serious' Buddhist also because he sees the comedy in human affairs. 'Tragic synchronicities are only funny to me,' he claims. It would be wrong to take this laughter as a lack of insight and compassion. No, the laughter always contains a hint of defiance. After suffering acutely from a second herniated disc, he understands that 'the absence of pain [is] a deception to be enjoyed ironically, with a mental sneer.' Like Bonny Hicks, perhaps like some of us living through this pandemic, he understands that health is merely the slowest possible rate at which one can die. When Wong comes face to face with death, he wants to greet it with a laugh: 'Is this all you've got? Is this all?'

The Shining Beam

Miracle of Mexico, Alfonso Reyes, translated by Timothy Adès (Shearsman) £14.95
Reviewed by Brian Morton

In April 1962, John Kennedy hosted a group of Nobel Prize-winners at an Executive Mansion dinner with a studiedly gracious introduction: 'I think this is the most extraordinary collection of talent, of human knowledge, that has ever been gathered together at the White House – with the possible exception of when Thomas Jefferson dined alone'. Those who knew and admired Alfonso Reyes had formed the same impression of him. Octavio Paz, who like Reyes served as a Mexican diplomat abroad, called him a 'collection of writers'. Paz got his Nobel Prize and was reportedly somewhat guilty that Reyes, who died in 1959, did not.

The sheer scale and depth of his writing suggests that he must have been a candidate, but maybe hampered in the committee's eyes by being known better as a journalist and literary investigator and less as a poet. Timothy Adès helps to address and correct that misperception with this marvellous collection. In privileging the Spanish texts on the right-hand, he quite rightly draws attention first to the very precise music of Reyes's verse, which often challenges effective translation. Right from the start, one notices that Adès strives to balance sense with a convincing English cadence: in 'To Cuernavaca', which is rendered in the English version as both 'Cuauhnáhuac!' and 'Cowhorn City!', he replaces Reyes' full stops with semi-colons and renders '*trina la urraca / y el laurerl de los pájaros murmura; // vuela una nube; un astro se destaca' / y el tiempo mismo se suspende y dura...*', as 'The magpie's ditty / trills, and the laurel bushes hum // with birds; a star is standing proud; / time stands suspended, stopped: a cloud / flies by', which takes some chances and just about gets away with them, though the notion of a magpie trilling a ditty is a stretch. To be fair, Adès walks in some forbidding footsteps. One of the first Anglophone writers to translate Reyes was Samuel Beckett.

'To Cuernavaca' comes at the beginning of *Homer en Cuernavaca*, an artfully random sequence of sonnets in which Reyes attempts to Hellenize Mexico; brilliantly wrought verses like 'Los exégetas' ('The Exegetes') are so finely rhymed that the English translator can only hang on for dear life and accept a certain compromise: '*Que el Janto absorba y beba en su camino / tal afluente, ye se revuelva el manto, en qué perturba la unidad del Jano, / en qué lo deja a menos cristalino?*' becomes 'If Xanthus in his bed receives / a stream, and ruckles up his sleeves, / does Xanthus spoil his unity, / or spoke his crystal purity?'. Where else to go with this?

The Homeric poems were written around 1948. A year later, in a letter quoted on the rear jacket of *Miracle Of Mexico*, Paz was writing to an associate, hailing Reyes as a man consumed by and wholly devoted to language. That is certainly the impression one takes from the poems, which never seem occasional or spontaneous, but almost ritualistically exact in their registration. Here and there, borrowing sometimes concepts he would have found in Benedetto Croce, he offers glimpses of an aesthetic manifesto. One later poem explicitly promises 'Consejo poético', and Adès gets the tone of its second stanza just right:

> Emotion? Ask the number,
> world-mover, primal governor.
> Temper the sacred instrument
> on the far side of sentiment.
> Discard the dumb, the deaf,
> the anxious and the rough.
> No need to fear it, far from it,
> if by the shining beam
> of some bright star or comet
> you can compact the track
> of your especial dream.

This is superbly done and it comes as close as one may to a summing-up of Reyes's brilliance. And for once the word is justified; the poetry has a high Mediterranean gleam and a lens-like clarity that could easily have been lost by careless rendering. Adès has done a great service.

No Wand Then

This Is Then, That Was Now, Vijay Seshadri (Graywolf) $24.00
Reviewed by Paul Franz

Born in Bangalore, India, and raised in Ohio and Pennsylvania, the poet and essayist Vijay Seshadri has now, decades after an itinerant youth in the Pacific Northwest, the settled restlessness of the New Yorker. (He lives in Brooklyn and teaches at Sarah Lawrence, in Yonkers.) 'I'll meet you if you really want to meet,' a speaker in his new book declares, 'But I won't meet for long, / and not for a minute will I look at you in your isolation, / your human isolation.' The proverbial New York minute is not to be given lightly. Why not? Because 'Looking at yours makes me look at mine – / transparencies of each other are they, yours and mine – / and I don't have time for mine, so how could I have time for yours?'

Seshadri is a poet of uneasy rumination, with several distinct but related styles: digressive meditations in long, loose lines; prose 'memory fragments'; and shorter poems in stanzas, often casually rhymed. These styles share a plainness and an elusiveness. Consider the new book's centerpiece, an elegy for the poet's father. Its first section, written in the meditative style Seshadri has traced to Ashbery and Wordsworth, draws an extended inverse comparison between the elegy's subject and a river. (Likely the Staunton River in Virginia, recalling the immigrant father and son's shared obsession with the American Civil War, recounted elsewhere.) 'Never not meaning what you said, never not transparent,' Seshadri writes, 'Never could you have been like this river, / acquiescent to, and companionable with, Earth, / supple, reconciled, patient...' And so on, over many sinuous lines, sentence and river parting company only when the former contrives, as the latter cannot, to 'bottom out' in a fertile stretch of midland, 'fructifying among the farms'.

Twisting, various, yet earthbound, the river signifies indirection, yet seems not quite antithetical to the man who keeps close to the facts. For one thing, the portrait of the father recalls an earlier intuition of his son. 'Personal Essay', the sprawling final poem of Seshadri's previous collection, 2013's masterful *3 Sections*, unfolds from the perception that the objects of knowledge and experience 'don't *resemble* anything. They're just themselves, they're only themselves.' There, literalism was an intimation of death, to be desperately but not finally evaded. Here, family affinity – implied in its very denial – haunts the self as a fate. Both prompt abundant speech, undeceived and spellbinding.

This Is Then, That Was Now is a slimmer book than its predecessor: slimmer and more urgent. Stringent in self-examination, it declines the more fashionable forms of indictment. Its characteristic rhetorical device is the feigned omission, what George Puttenham called 'Paralepsis; or The Passager'. What one *could* but officially does not say; what one *might* but (for now) does not do: such shadows are the poems' substance. Their heroes are solitaries, cherishing yet compromised by their own separateness. A film noir 'private eye' savors a typical double bind: 'There is an innocence / to establish and an anguish in / him he needs to destroy / before it destroys him, an / anguish so pure it almost / feels like joy.'

Time passes: you become me; we become nothing. Seshadri's vision offers no escape. Then again, its obliquity does not require one. The 'vacuum of perpetual space', one poem proposes, is 'a blackbird'. Be sure not to miss 'its black eye, black in black, / its sidewise look that makes you / look back

'Why go straight?'

The Craft of Poetry, Lucy Newlyn (Yale University Press) £14.99
Reviewed by Ian Brinton

In the introduction to *The Craft of Poetry* the teacher, academic and poet Lucy Newlyn focuses our attention upon the poetic process of 'seeing the familiar world in new ways'. The intriguing quality of the book is that rather than providing an analysis of a range of poems through which the reader can be guided in order to become aware of the wide diversity of poetic art, from metaphor to allegory, from personification to litotes and from ode to epitaph, Newlyn presents one hundred and thirty-five of her own poems in an engaging pattern that moves us from the particular to the general. We are guided on a compelling journey in which the poems speak for themselves and in which each individual component contributes to the whole picture. We are inevitably reminded of the words from Edward Thomas which Newlyn had used as an epigraph to her deeply reflective collection of poems, *Ginnel*, which was published by Carcanet in 2005: 'Why go straight? There is nothing at the end of any road better than may be found beside it, though there would be no travel, did men believe it.' In a way not dissimilar to the manner in which the Swiss poet Philippe Jaccottet has referred to 'ouvertures', those rents in the fabric of what surrounds us which enable us to see a new world, Newlyn's journey of discovery and presentation begins in the world of 'a remembered place' and becomes 'a handbook guiding the reader in the art of writing/reading poetry'.

The pattern in which words are placed on a page is inseparable from meaning and as we are told in the fourth poem of the sequence, 'Without edge, form would be invisible, /

almost inaudible – like muffled shapes and sounds in mist.' Newlyn is aware from the very start of this journey that we steer ourselves towards the edges of things in order to recognise them and she succeeds in what Charles Tomlinson had referred to in 'Aesthetic', one of his early poems from the 1950s: 'Reality is to be sought, not in concrete, / But in space made articulate'.

The poems are set in Appersett, a small village in Wensleydale, where Lucy Newlyn spent much of her childhood and the 'beck', the winding stream of the Widdale, provides the structure for the journey. As readers we listen 'for the beck's spirit / in its voice' and also 'watch for it / in the dancing line on the page' and that focus upon sound echoes a much earlier account of poetic art, George Puttenham's *The Arte of English Poesie* which had appeared in the early 1580s: 'For the eare is properly but an instrument of conveyance for the minde, to apprehend the sense by the sound.' Lucy Newlyn's journey through the world of prosody this quality of sound is heard throughout in a manner that is hauntingly evocative and her own example of a villanelle reveals how the critic who is herself a poet can teach the art by bringing it to life:

A silken thread unwinding from a
  spool,
a curlew circling on the farthest fell,
clear water falling in a deep green
  pool.

A winding path through beech
  trees, fresh and cool,
a sea of bluebells in a hidden dell,
a silken thread unwinding from a
  spool.

Threading its way through the six stanzas of the poem we hear the echoing sound in 'Rhyme's chalice' and the whole construct becomes 'soft-ocean music trapped inside a shell'. Like the child who holds a shell to the ear in order to hear the sound of distant oceans we are presented with the truth of Puttenham's assertion concerning the ear as we gaze upon the image of a long summer of 'unending leisure' which is as 'deep as any well'. In her 'Villanelle' Lucy Newlyn captures those echoes which were so central to the work of Edward Thomas, that awareness of something on the edge of consciousness which F.R. Leavis had suggested would disappear if looked at directly:

> Rhyme's measure, the wise poet's
>   craft and tool:
> the sweet sad beauty of a villanelle,
> a silken thread unwinding from a
>   spool,
> clear water falling in a deep green
>   pool.

Endless Present

Cargo of Limbs, Martyn Crucefix
(Hercules Editions) £10
Grammar of Passage, Monika Cassel
(Flap) £4
Reviewed by Rory Waterman

In our cultural moment, we are fervently encouraged – by corporations, much of the media, some politicians and definitely not others – to focus (often superficially) on certain kinds of inequality at home, or in America. Others are routinely ignored. So, often, are the lessons we might learn from the past. And so, increasingly, is whatever is happening anywhere else in the world, however awful it might be. In this review, I want to draw attention to two pamphlets that engage perceptively and meaningfully with, respectively, fraught places and times that are not our own. We might learn from thinking about them, but these pamphlets are the work of poets, not proselytisers, and what we take from their works is up to us.

Martyn Crucefix's *Cargo of Limbs*, a long poem in sometimes disorientingly short-lined quatrains, takes as inspiration Aeneas's journey into the Underworld in Book VI of the *Aenead* to depict the plights of Syrian refugees in the Mediterranean during the refugee crisis that we are now implicitly encouraged to believe has ended. The narrator is an on-scene photojournalist who, at the end of the poem, is relieved of his camera by Andras – the poem's Aeneas? – who is also a journalist:

> I raise my camera still
>
> he lifts his feeble hand
> and by what rule say
> by what moral right
> does he smash it to the ground

The narrator is a coolly objective character, eye to viewfinder, and Andras a man of empathy. The narrative is caught between two ways of witnessing and recording, as well as between recording and experiencing. It is frenetic, purposefully confused in places, a running set of fragmentations, and hard to focus on in one sitting – though it begs to be read that way, and at a speed to induce anxiety:

> she pummels her breasts
> on his cheek yellow dust
> of poison breeze running
>
> into the trunks of trees
> suddenly blind shrieking
> before the militia –
> shaken from mattress
>
> Old Age scarcely able
> forced at gunpoint
> a pink nightdress hurried
> under tarpaulins on flat-
>
> bed trucks eyes steeled

I am not convinced the poem would work very well on its own: this sort of writing, emotive though it can be and in this case often is, can all too easily seem like a banal thought exercise, untethered emotionally to the circumstances that occasioned it. However, *Cargo of Limbs* is a particularly successful multimedia collaboration, and the poem is shown to best advantage. Hercules Editions pamphlets are beautiful little square booklets, just long enough to be perfect-bound. The poems they publish are always matched with the work of visual artists – in this case, often clandestine-seeming, often awkward-angled stills from the superb documentary *Purple Sea* (2019). As Amel Alzacout, who took them, says in an endnote to the volume, 'I had with me' – at the Turkish port city of Izmir and on a 'small wooden boat' intended for Lesbos – 'an action camera which I tied to my wrist and hid under my jacket sleeve. Smugglers usually confiscate mobile phones or cameras if they spot someone filming'. In apparently out-of-sequence images we see queues of apparent would-be migrants as shadows, a tantalising view of Greece from a dusty concrete harbour wall, the boat filling with sparkling seawater. It is the perfect accompaniment, from an artist apparently poised between the perspectives of the poem's two main characters.

There are many frenetic moments too in the American poet Monika Cassel's debut pamphlet, *Grammar of Passage*. The opening poem, 'Arrival', is one long sentence of impressions and movement:

> a kiss on my grandmothers' cheek
> – high up and surprisingly soft
> in the face with the stern eyes,
> forbidding lips – white-tablecloth
> lunch of Kassler Rippchen und
> Sauerkraut on the balcony with a
> quick sip of mother's beer, barges
> puttering coal-smoke along the
> Rhine below, and a nap behind the
> rattling jalousies that admit only
> particles of afternoon light [...]

What follows is a series of ten poems, each an atmospheric glimpse of a family caught up in Nazi Germany and its aftermath, and each dated to between 1941 and 1956, with two further poems set in the twenty-first century at the end. Several are presented as what might be directions for a screenplay:

> Cut to a boy pulling a dachshund
>   on a leash,
> cut to soldiers
> marching ten Russian POWs down
>   the street.
>
>   On the street, deep-gabled
> houses.
>
> Cut to the kids who play
> in the dirt lane by the iron fence,
> to my mother, two years old,
> rubbing her eyes (she's crying),

her flowered pinafore
fastened over her sweater.

This style almost eliminates editori-
alising, of course, and allows Cassel
to present emotive circumstances as
unencumbered as possible by the
contexts in which we usually put
them. We are never told what to
think, but are instead encouraged to
understand that the quotidian
aspects of life might be harder for
some to navigate than almost any of
us can imagine. We sympathise with
the family, though at the same time
we can never quite be sure of the
extent of their complicity. In 'Thrift,
ca. 1946',

She made me a new red dress
when the schools opened again:
pulled the old flag out from a
    drawer,
clipped the stitches
from the circle in the center, held
    it up [...]
A lot of girls wear red
these days.

The last two poems maroon all of
this in the uncanny past. In the title
poem, subtitled 'train through south
Germany', we move through 'ances-
tral fields' and 'past a brewery, past
warehouses', speeding 'towards,
away, unknown – / each second we
articulate, it changes':

Everything's punctuation, a *there*
and *there* and *there*,
    the apple trees arrayed across a
hill,
    the now now now of the pigeons
who strut the city platform
    an endless present, heads a-bob-
bing as they range:
    They're here, they change.

It's not perfect, is it? 'That', not
'who', would be preferable grammati-
cally – the irony! – and surely 'bob-
bing' would do on its own. But it is
still vivid, and emotionally complex,
and truthfully unresolved.

Contributors

Linda Stern Zisquit has published five full-length poetry collections, most recently *Return from Elsewhere and Havoc: New & Selected Poems*. Her pamphlet "From the Notebooks of Korah's Daughter" was published in 2019 by New Walk Editions. **J. Kates** is a poet and literary translator who lives in Fitzwilliam, New Hampshire. **Sam Milne** has recently published a series of plays in the Scots magazine, *Lallans*. He has just completed a translation of the *Iliad* in Scots, and translations of Racine's *Andromaque* and Sophocles's *Antigone*. **Beverley Bie Brahic**'s *White Sheets* (CBe) was a finalist for the Forward Prize. Her latest books are *The Hotel Eden* (Carcanet) and *Baudelaire: Invitation to the Voyage* (Seagull Books). A Canadian she lives in Paris. **Lisa Kelly**'s first collection, *A Map Towards Fluency* is published by Carcanet. Her latest pamphlet, From the *IKEA Back Catalogue* is published by New Walk Editions. She is studying British Sign Language. **Sujata Bhatt** has published nine collections of poetry with Carcanet including a *Selected* and a *Collected Poems*. In spring 2020 she was the inaugural writer in residence at the Bauhaus Foundation in Dessau, Germany. **Yousif M. Qasmiyeh** is a doctoral researcher at the University of Oxford. His collection, *Writing the Camp* (Broken Sleep Books, 2021), was The Poetry Book Society's Recommendation for Spring 2021. **Irina Mashinski** is the author of ten books of poetry in Russian. She is co-editor, with Robert Chandler and Boris Dralyuk, of *The Penguin Book of Russian Poetry* and of the *Cardinal Points Journal*. Her first book in English, *The Naked World*, is forthcoming from MadHat Press in the fall of 2021.

Colophon

Editors
Michael Schmidt
John McAuliffe

Editorial Manager
Andrew Latimer

Contributing Editors
Vahni Capildeo
Sasha Dugdale
Will Harris

Design
Cover and Layout
by Emily Benton Book Design

Editorial address
The Editors at the address on the right. Manuscripts cannot be returned unless accompanied by a stamped addressed envelope or international reply coupon.

Trade distributors
NBN International

Represented by
Compass ips Ltd

Copyright
© 2021 Poetry Nation Review
All rights reserved
ISBN 978-1-78410-839-7
ISBN 0144-7076

Subscriptions—6 issues
INDIVIDUAL–print and digital:
£39.50; abroad £49
INSTITUTIONS–print only:
£76; abroad £90
INSTITUTIONS–digital only:
from Exact Editions (https://shop.exacteditions.com/gb/pn-review)
to: PN Review, Alliance House, 30 Cross Street, Manchester, M2 7AQ, UK.

Supported by